Against the Ice
The Story of December 1776

True stories of
Pennsylvania & Pennsylvanians
in the American Revolutionary War

JOHN L. MOORE

Mechanicsburg, PA USA

Published by Sunbury Press, Inc.
Mechanicsburg, Pennsylvania

SUNBURY
www.sunburypress.com

Copyright © 2020 by John L. Moore.
Cover Copyright © 2020 by Sunbury Press, Inc.

Sunbury Press supports copyright. Copyright fuels creativity, encourages diverse voices, promotes free speech, and creates a vibrant culture. Thank you for buying an authorized edition of this book and for complying with copyright laws by not reproducing, scanning, or distributing any part of it in any form without permission. You are supporting writers and allowing Sunbury Press to continue to publish books for every reader. For information contact Sunbury Press, Inc., Subsidiary Rights Dept., PO Box 548, Boiling Springs, PA 17007 USA or legal@sunburypress.com.

For information about special discounts for bulk purchases, please contact Sunbury Press Orders Dept. at (855) 338-8359 or orders@sunburypress.com.

To request one of our authors for speaking engagements or book signings, please contact Sunbury Press Publicity Dept. at publicity@sunburypress.com.

FIRST SUNBURY PRESS EDITION: May 2020

Set in Adobe Garamond | Interior design by Crystal Devine | Cover by Lawrence Knorr | Edited by Lawrence Knorr.

Publisher's Cataloging-in-Publication Data
Names: Moore, John L., author.
Title: Against the ice : the story of december 1776 / John L. Moore.
Description: First trade paperback edition. | Mechanicsburg, PA : Sunbury Press, 2020.
Summary: Washington's crossing of the Delaware River on a cold Christmas night in 1776, followed by the successful attack on the Hessians at Trenton, was the turning point in the American Revolution and in Washington's career.
Identifiers: ISBN 978-1-620062-76-0 (softcover).
Subjects: HISTORY / United States / State & Local / Middle Atlantic | HISTORY / United States / Revolutionary Period (1775-1800).

Product of the United States of America
0 1 1 2 3 5 8 13 21 34 55

Continue the Enlightenment!

In memoriam

Charles Pidcock of Coryell's Ferry (Lambertville), New Jersey. He enlisted on July 4, 1776, in Captain John Phillips's Company, Colonel David Chambers' Third Regiment, Hunterdon County Militia. A paternal ancestor.

And

Christopher Hite of Bedford, Pennsylvania. He enlisted in the Continental Army on April 23, 1777. He served in Captain John Wilkins' Company, Colonel Oliver Spencer's Additional Regiment, Continental Army. A maternal ancestor.

Both soldiers fought on the American side at the Battle of Germantown near Philadelphia on October 4, 1777. It is doubtful that they knew each other.

Other books in the
Revolutionary Pennsylvania series:

Tories, Terror, and Tea

Scorched Earth: General Sullivan and the Senecas

1780: Year of Revenge

Contents

Acknowledgments vii

Author's Note. ix

Against the Ice 1

Selected Bibliography. 109

About the Author. 111

Acknowledgments

Jane E. Moore and Robert B. Swift read the manuscript and suggested improvements. Jane and Robert accompanied me on visits to many of the places mentioned in the narrative.

About the cover

A detail from *The Passage of the Delaware*, a painting by Thomas Sully (1783–1872) showing General George Washington as he watches the Continental Army cross the Delaware River in December 1776. The painting is part of the collection of the Museum of Fine Arts, Boston.

Author's Note

I approach the many stories of the American Revolutionary War as a journalist. My mission lies in presenting the soldiers of the Revolution and their contemporaries in their own words and in a way that gives modern readers a sense of immediacy with people who lived more than two centuries ago. To accomplish this, I draw on soldiers' journals, letters, memoirs, and other first-person sources.

I have occasionally omitted phrases or sentences from quotations and have employed an ellipsis (. . .) to indicate where I have done so. In some instances, I have modernized spelling and punctuation.

John L. Moore
Northumberland, Pennsylvania
March 2020

Against the Ice
on December 25, 1776

Down from Durham,
And up from Bordentown,
These long boats came,
Collected, guarded,
Near McKonkey's
On the Delaware's
Western shore.

Eight feet wide,
And sixty long,
These flat-bottoms
On their regular runs
Shipped pig iron,
Oats and wheat
Flour in barrels
Or in cloth sacks,
Even whiskey in jugs.

But tonight
Washington meant
Each one to haul
A regiment
Of shoeless soldiers,

Of shivering patriots,
Their feet wrapped
In rags for warmth,
Their powder getting wet
From blowing snow.

Despite the current,
The seasoned sailors
At the oars propelled
The long boats eastward
Toward New Jersey.
Their wooden hulls
Creaked and groaned
As the sailors
Forced them
Against the ice.

Downstream, Trenton
unknowingly awaited.

Sunday, November 24

'Come by a safe and secure route'

General Washington warned Major General Charles Lee on Sunday, November 24, 1776, that the British were actively looking for him.

"By direct intelligence from their camp, I am informed that... measures are taking to intercept your march," Washington said.

Lee's division, which included several Continental regiments, was camped east of the Hudson River in New York's Westchester County. Lee was some thirty miles north of New York, then a small town of about twenty-five thousand people, located at the bottom of Manhattan Island. The British and their Hessian auxiliaries occupied the entire island and controlled the bridges that linked upper Manhattan with the mainland to the north and the roads leading to Westchester.

Writing to Lee from Newark, Washington had already crossed the Hudson into New Jersey and had begun a slow retreat across New Jersey, one that would soon take the Continental Army to Trenton and across the Delaware River into Pennsylvania.

Now that he knew the British intended to capture Lee, Washington said, "I must request that you will take every precaution to come by a safe and secure route."

A professional soldier for two decades, Lee had been an officer in the British Army before the American Revolution, and Washington regarded him as a military asset that neither he nor the Continental Army could afford to lose. In turn, the British viewed Lee as a traitor.

During the French and Indian War, Lee had served as a captain in the 44th Foot, a British infantry regiment that saw action at the Battle of the Monongahela in 1755 and the Battle of Ticonderoga three years later. After the war, he had also served as an officer in the armies of Portugal and Poland. Lee had held the rank of major when he retired from the British service in the early 1770s.

Nobody else on the American side had that much military experience. Indeed, when the fighting began in Massachusetts in April 1775, most colonists had been farmers, tradesmen, and merchants. Few had ever belonged to a military organization—those who had mostly belonged to local militias that had practiced drilling on the village green.

From the Battle of Long Island in August to the captures of Forts Washington and Lee in November, General William Howe's soldiers had consistently battered Washington's army, which had begun to disintegrate. With winter approaching, Washington saw that significant numbers of his soldiers were deserting.

In mid-November, when Washington ordered his army to leave New York State and regroup west of the Hudson River in New Jersey, the enemy followed.

By Thursday, November 21, Washington had reached Hackensack, New Jersey, and was beginning to move south when he ordered Lee to join him.

"We have not above three thousand men, and they much broken and dispirited," Washington told Lee. He added, "The public interest requires your coming over to this side with the Continental troops."

Lee had a larger army. During the second week of November, Washington told Hancock that he had shifted

General George Washington

a sizeable force from New York to New Jersey to oppose "any incursions the enemy may attempt in this neighborhood." Washington himself had arrived at present-day Fort Lee, New Jersey, on November 13. Lee remained in Westchester County to discourage any British advance north of Manhattan. Lee commanded seven thousand soldiers, author Dominick Mazzagetti noted in *Charles Lee: Self Before Country*.

By Sunday, November 24, Washington had moved sixteen miles south to Newark, but Lee remained in Westchester. In a letter, Washington told Lee that he should join his army in New Jersey. The commander underscored "the necessity of your gaining intelligence of the enemy's situation in the course of your march," and requested that Lee send "frequent expresses to advise of your approaches." Washington closed by expressing hope and trust "that your arrival will be safe and happy."

Two days later, on Tuesday, November 26, Lee informed Washington that he remained east of the Hudson River at

General Charles Lee

Camp Phillipsburg (presumably present-day Hartsdale in Westchester), but would presently leave for New Jersey—"I set out tomorrow"—and "I shall take care to obey your Excellency's order in regard to my march as exactly as possible."

Lee's reply displeased Washington. "I confess I expected you would have been sooner in motion," Washington said in a response written at Newark on Wednesday, November 27. "The force here when joined by yours will not be adequate to any great opposition. At present, it is weak, and it has been more owing to the badness of the weather that the enemy's progress has been checked than any resistance we could make. They are now pushing this way."

Washington's letters make it clear that he expected regular updates from Lee, but many days passed before Washington received any word from him at all. As Washington and the main Continental Army pushed farther and farther into New Jersey, Washington realized that he had lost contact with Lee and didn't know where Lee had taken his army.

If Washington didn't know Lee's whereabouts, he knew all too well where the British army was. It was right behind him. He reacted by leading the Continental Army in full retreat in a march that, for days, took his soldiers from Newark to New Brunswick, Kingston, Princeton, Trenton, and, finally, across the Delaware into Pennsylvania's Bucks County.

By Sunday, December 1, the Americans had limped their way to New Brunswick, nearly thirty miles south of Newark.

"The enemy are still advancing," Washington said in a letter written that day to Hancock. "Some say they were joined yesterday by a considerable reinforcement from Staten Island. How far this fact may be true, I cannot determine, but from every information before, they were between six and seven thousand strong."

Washington saw little merit in making a stand at the Raritan River. "Without a sufficient number of men and arms, their progress cannot be checked," the general told Hancock. "At present, our force is totally inadequate to any attempt."

What's more, the combined force of Hessians and British was coming Hancock's way. "I have for some time past supposed Philadelphia to be the object of their movement and have every reason to believe my opinion well-founded," the general said.

Washington had previously alerted Hancock to his increasingly desperate need for reinforcements. To help in achieving this, Washington had sent Brigadier General Thomas Mifflin to Philadelphia in late November to persuade Congress to provide both reinforcements and pay for the soldiers already in service. The congressmen responded by issuing an emergency call for militia troops to race to Washington's aid.

"The German Battalion move from hence tomorrow," Mifflin had reported to Washington on Tuesday, November 26. "Three regiments from Delaware and Maryland are to follow them to Brunswick as soon as possible . . . The light horse of the state of Virginia are ordered to join your Excellency's army."

The Congress also urged the government of Pennsylvania to call out the militia for Philadelphia, Bucks, Chester, and Northampton counties.

Mifflin added that he had ordered a thousand wagons to haul provisions and supplies. The supplies would include "five hundred thousand musket cartridges (which) will be sent to Brunswick."

The Congress remained woefully short of money to pay the troops, but Mifflin reported a windfall had occurred. "A prize ship came in yesterday," Mifflin disclosed. "She had on board, when taken by a Congress packet, twenty thousand hard (dollars) nine thousand of which were lost by an attempt (to heave) them on board the packet at sea."

As Washington neared the Delaware River, Pennsylvania troops began leaving the army in droves. To discourage this, Washington asked the governor of New Jersey, William Livingston, to post guards along all the roads leading to Pennsylvania and at all the ferries that crossed the Delaware River.

"Although most of the Pennsylvanians are enlisted till the 1st of January, I am informed that they are deserting in great numbers," Washington told Livingston. He asked the governor to order "the officers of militia on the roads and the ferries over Delaware to take up and secure every soldier that has not a regular discharge or pass."

Sunday, December 1

'Secure the Durham boats on the Delaware'

The commanding general also ordered Brigadier General William Maxwell of New Jersey and Colonel Richard Humpton of Pennsylvania to hurry to the Delaware and have their men gather up all the boats they could find. He also sent soldiers to Trenton with orders to collect lumber along the Delaware's east shore and to begin building rafts–as many as they could.

Writing to Governor Livingston on Sunday, December 1, from New Brunswick, Washington reported that Howe's soldiers were "impressing wagons and horses, and collecting cattle and sheep, which is a further proof of their intent to march a considerable distance." He warned that "unless my force is speedily augmented," his numbers would be too small "for me to make any stand at this place, when the enemy advance, as I have not, including General Williamson's militia (say one thousand) more than four thousand men."

The general repeated his conviction that "the boats and craft all along the Delaware . . . should be secured, particularly the Durham boats used for the transportation of produce down the river. (Militia) parties should be sent to all the landings to have them removed to the other side, hauled up and put under proper guards."

By Tuesday, December 3, Washington reached Trenton. He concentrated on the task at hand: moving his remaining men and material across the Delaware as rapidly as possible. "A great quantity are already got over," he said, "and as soon as the boats come up from Philadelphia, we shall load them, by which means I hope to have everything secured this night and tomorrow if we are not disturbed."

But Washington also continued to puzzle over the whereabouts of General Lee. "I have not heard a word from General Lee since the 26th (of) last month, which surprises me not a little," Washington told Hancock. ". . . I have dispatched daily expresses to him desiring to know when I might look for him."

The lack of news from Lee was becoming a cause for alarm. Washington had expected that when Lee joined the main army, he would arrive with "several Continental regiments in his division." Since leaving Westchester, Lee's force may have grown significantly. "I am informed by report that General (Arthur) St. Clair has joined him with three or four regiments from the Northward." Washington said that he had sent a reliable officer out "to know the truth of this."

A letter that Washington sent to Lee from New Brunswick on December 1 had generated a tardy response. "The force I have with me is infinitely inferior in number and such as cannot give or promise the least successful opposition," Washington had said.

Lee's reply was dated December 8. "I am extremely shocked to hear that your force is so inadequate to the necessity of your situation—as I had been taught to think you had been considerably re-enforced," Lee said.

The errant general by now had reached Chatham, a New Jersey village about twenty-five miles north of New Brunswick, but Washington and the main army had already arrived at Trenton and were crossing into Pennsylvania's Bucks County. Lee's division was now more than fifty miles north of Washington's army.

On Sunday, December 1, British troops had suddenly appeared opposite New Brunswick, across the Raritan River. An artillery unit–tradition says it was made up of Kings College students from Manhattan and commanded by Captain Alexander Hamilton—fired its cannons at the advancing enemy. At the same time, other Continentals tried vainly to destroy the bridge spanning the river.

"The enemy appeared in view at 1 o'clock," Sergeant James McMichael of the Pennsylvania Rifle Regiment wrote in his journal. "We were all under arms on the parade. Immediately a heavy cannonade commenced on both sides, which continued an hour in which we had two killed." The bridge hadn't been destroyed by the time the Americans were ordered "to evacuate the town, and so proceeded towards Princeton and encamped near Kingston," said McMichael, a Scot who had emigrated to Pennsylvania and had been living in Lancaster when hostilities erupted with Britain.

Washington's forces raced toward Princeton, sixteen miles south of New Brunswick and fourteen miles north of Trenton. The general himself reached Princeton in time for breakfast on Monday, December 2, then pressed on to Trenton and arrived by noon.

General Charles Cornwallis

The British field commander, Lord Charles Cornwallis, briefly halted his advance at New Brunswick, a move that let the Pennsylvania riflemen remain at Princeton. This village struck Sergeant McMichael as "somewhat beautiful" even if its inhabitants happened to be "chiefly Tories."

On Wednesday, December 4, "We now received undoubted intelligence that the enemy is advancing, which occasioned the inhabitants to remove their most valuable effects to Pennsylvania," about fifteen miles to the southwest, the sergeant said.

The Pennsylvania riflemen also fell back to Trenton. As McMichael noted in his journal for Sunday, December 8: "We paraded in Trenton at 4 A.M., and at dawn crossed the ferry into Pennsylvania. At 4 P.M., the Hessians appeared in view but were soon dispersed by several messengers sent from an eighteen-pounder of ours from the shore. Here we remained in the woods, having neither blankets or tents."

Monday, December 2

The British approach, alarm Philadelphia

Philadelphians panicked on Monday, December 2, when they learned that the British, apparently headed for their city, had already chased Washington half-way across New Jersey. "This city alarmed with the news of Howe's army's being at Brunswick, proceeding for this place," reported Christopher Marshall, a retired Philadelphia druggist. "Drums beat, a martial appearance, the shops shut, and all business—except preparing to disappoint our enemies—laid aside."

A staunch patriot, Marshall knew—and kept in nearly daily contact with—many of the city's revolutionary leaders and thus kept abreast of the increasing threat posed by the British.

On Tuesday, December 3, Marshall wrote that he saw "numbers of families loading wagons with their furniture and taking them out of town." Keeping a cool head, Marshall realized that the time for precautions had arrived. "Drank tea at home," he wrote, "then went with a number of deeds to son Christopher's. Put them into his iron chest. No news to be depended upon."

Two days later, Philadelphia's militiamen began heading up the Delaware River to reinforce the Continentals at Trenton.

Sergeant William Young reported that on Thursday, December 5, his company of wagoners "set out by water from Philadelphia in a schooner for Trenton . . . to oppose General Howe . . . Reached Bristol by two o'clock, went on shore, and marched to Trenton. Got there by night. Met with some difficulty to get a lodging." The soldiers eventually went to the residence of a Mr. Brown, "who kindly let us lodge in his stove room."

Apparently, there was some thought given to marching the Philadelphia militia twelve miles inland to take up positions at Princeton, but on Saturday, December 7, Washington advised Colonel John Cadwalader, a Philadelphian who commanded these troops, "I would have you remain here till the whole of your brigade comes up." The general wanted these troops provided with ammunition and "regularly supplied with three days' provisions, ready cooked, that they may be ready to march at a moment's warning."

Also, on the 7th came "orders to move our quarters and retreat over Delaware on account of "Howe's advance party . . . near at hand," Sergeant Young reported. The company crossed into Bucks County after nightfall "and lay on the shore very cold—and with much difficulty got some wood to make a fire." The sergeant noted that he "renewed a cold I got coming up the river."

Monday, December 9

A major's quest for shirts, shoes for his men

On Monday, December 9, the day after the soldiers in Sergeant McMichael's regiment crossed into Bucks County, the men hiked about five miles upriver.

As the sergeant reported in his journal, "At 3 P.M. we marched from near Trenton ferry to Thompson's Mill near Coryell's Ferry (present-day New Hope), where we encamped in the woods. Weather very cold." Within a few days, hundreds of soldiers had camped around the mill.

"Here we were situate(d) on the bank of Delaware thirty-three miles from Philadelphia and twelve from Trenton," McMichael added. "We thus remained for several days without anything occurring worthy of record. The inhabitants are Quakers and mean to maintain a strict neutrality in the present unhappy contest . . ."

McMichael was a sergeant in Captain John Marshall's company, which was part of the 2nd Battalion, which in turn belonged to Colonel Samuel Miles's Pennsylvania Rifle Regiment.

As a sixteen-year-old volunteer from Lancaster in 1756, Miles had served under General Benjamin Franklin in eastern Pennsylvania during the French and Indian War. Two decades later, his career as colonel of the rifle regiment lasted little more than five months. It began when the regiment was organized in March 1776 and ended on August 27 when Hessian soldiers captured him at the Battle of Long Island.

In writing about the battle years later, Miles said that he became separated from his battalions following a firefight and attempted to hide in a wood. "I was myself entirely cut off from our lines and therefore endeavored to conceal myself, with a few men who would not leave me," Miles said. "I hoped to remain until night . . . but about 3 o'clock in the afternoon was discovered by a party of Hessians and obliged to surrender." Hundreds of Americans were captured, wounded, or killed during the battle, which the British won.

When Lieutenant Colonel James Piper, a Bedford soldier who commanded the regiment's 1st Battalion, was also captured that day, command of the battalion passed to Major Ennion Williams. The major accompanied the battalion to Thompson's Mill.

As the riflemen set up camp, Williams quickly resumed his months-long, persistent campaign to obtain clothing for them. "They want shirts, shoes, breeches, waistcoats, coats, and stockings, and about fifty blankets," Williams said in a mid-December letter to Pennsylvania officials in Philadelphia. Several days later, when he failed to receive what he regarded as an adequate response, he warned that the shortage of clothing might well render his troops unfit for duty.

Documents dating to the autumn of 1776 show that Williams had begun a months' long effort to secure blankets and warm clothing for the riflemen before winter set in. In an October 7 letter, the major noted that in late summer, "a large quantity of blankets"—"I believe two bales"—intended for the Pennsylvanians had been shipped to Fort Constitution (later known as Fort Lee) overlooking Upper Manhattan on the New Jersey side of the Hudson River. "There, through mistake of the assistant deputy quartermaster general, they were opened and distributed to (other soldiers) . . . so that our suffering troops did not receive any."

Addressing Thomas Wharton, the head of the Pennsylvania Council of Safety, the major also asked "whether the clothes . . . belonging to those soldiers missing on Long Island are to be appraised and delivered to the troops at camp?"

As the Continentals reached New Brunswick in late November, Major Williams again wrote to the Council of Safety. In a Saturday, November 30, letter to a council member, Colonel Owen Biddle, Williams said he had learned that "clothing for the regiment is now ready. I have acquainted Lord Stirling, in whose brigade our regiment is, and he directs that they remain in Philadelphia until further orders." The major added that "the enemy are advancing by slow and secure movements, but as soon as our Pennsylvania and Jersey militia join us, I hope to convince them that we can and will disperse them."

By Thursday, December 12, the Pennsylvania regiment had settled around the farm and gristmill of Robert Thompson. Lord Stirling had moved into Thompson's fieldstone house, which sat on the bank of Pidcock Creek, a short distance from where it flowed into the Delaware. Major Williams wrote a series of letters that describe camp life and the variety of issues confronting the riflemen.

"Our regiment remains in twelve companies, consisting of about two hundred rank-and-file, sixteen or seventeen

Major General William Alexander, Lord Stirling, stayed in the Bucks County residence of miller Robert Thompson prior to the Battle of Trenton. Restored and open to the public, the building is known as the Thompson-Neely House and is part of Washington Crossing Historic Park.

sergeants, fourteen subalterns, and six captains, fit for duty, in good spirits, though thinly clad and penniless," Williams noted in a report to the Council of Safety. ". . . As soon as we know where we shall remain for a few days, it will be very happy for our regiment to be supplied with clothes and part of their pay, at least."

The major acknowledged that there was always the chance that Howe's army "will attempt a landing" in Pennsylvania. Still, he downplayed the possibility that the British or Hessians would be able to land anywhere near the Continental encampment. "We are destroying or sinking every boat or means of transporting troops to this shore," William said. He added: "It is my opinion that the enemy will be prevented from reaching this side of Delaware this year. The prisoners that have lately been taken are very ragged, and no doubt, the enemy will be severely pinched by the cold."

Williams also expressed concern about several soldiers in his battalion who were absent without leave. The major singled out one officer, "Adjutant Wallace," for censure. The man "has not been with the regiment since we left Trenton Ferry, and if he joins the regiment again, he will be tried for his conduct. His absenting himself thus without leave at a time when we heard the enemy were landed on this shore and expected to go immediately to action is too gross behavior to pass unnoticed."

Two other officers, "Captain Farmer and Lieutenant Maise," had traveled to Philadelphia "with a complaint of the rheumatism. Perhaps by this time, they may be recovered and may collect a number of our men that are strolling in Philadelphia."

In a letter to the Council of Safety dated Friday, December 13, the major reported that "this morning Lord Stirling has been pleased to permit me to send for clothing for our regiment, and to have them paid off."

Williams was blunt in describing the Pennsylvanians: "The men are barefooted and very thinly clad, and have not received any pay these three months."

He also sent a letter to Biddle the same day requesting that the Philadelphian immediately ship "such clothing as you have ready, to the number of two hundred and thirty suits" to Thompson's Mill. He emphasized that the needs of "our poor distressed soldiers" were severe.

On Monday, December 16, writing again from Thompson's Mill, the major advised the Council of Safety that the paymaster had arrived in camp. He also reported that his troops needed the clothing the regiment had ordered several months earlier. "It will give me much satisfaction if I can get the three hundred suits you mention to be sent to Lord Stirling," Williams said. He disclosed that he knew "the suits made on purpose for them, which—I am too well informed—are to our mortification delivered out to other regiments."

The major said, "it is a mystery to me that this accident should . . . happen; however, amidst other matters, this is attempted to be laid at my door." Williams pointed out that he had written to the council from New Brunswick on Saturday, November 30, and "directed that they should remain in Philadelphia."

"It will, therefore, give me satisfaction to have the letter (I) wrote to you from Brunswick safely kept," Williams said.

Biddle responded by the next day and advised the major that he would send "such a number of the three hundred suits . . . as our regiment may want." That same day, the major informed the Council of Safety that Colonel Biddle "informs me that he has orders to permit no troops (except those enlisted . . . for three years) to have any shoes, stockings, or clothing, that may come to his care." The men in the rifle regiment had enlisted for a much shorter period.

Williams objected to Biddle's report. "Unless you provide shoes and stockings on purpose for our bare-footed men, and direct them to me, or obtain . . . permission from his Excellency that they may be delivered to us, it will be impossible for our regiment to do duty here much longer."

Documents contained in the Pennsylvania Archives indicate that the clothing needs of the soldiers at Thompson's Mill were snagged by governmental red tape. In early 1776, the Pennsylvania House of Representatives had created a special force of fifteen hundred soldiers. The Pennsylvania Rifle Regiment would consist of a thousand riflemen, divided into two battalions of five hundred men each. The other five hundred soldiers would belong to the Pennsylvania Battalion of Musketry. The legislation that authorized the formation of the regiment specified that the enlistments of these troops would expire at the end of January 1778. In other words, these enlistment periods weren't long enough to meet the requirements spelled out by Colonel Biddle. Therefore, Biddle couldn't supply them with any clothing, stockings, or shoes.

The soldiers desperately needed these items, and Major Williams was outraged that Biddle intended to obey his orders to the letter. His doing so would mean that "our men will, therefore, go barefooted unless . . . some other mode is pointed out."

Clothing for at least some of the riflemen was delivered to camp four days before Christmas. Some of it was new, and some, second-hand. As Williams explained in a Saturday, December 21, report to the Council of Safety, "The fifty-eight suits of new clothes, fifty-eight of old, the caps and shoes have come to hand and are distributing." But the shipment was incomplete: "The three hundred suits mentioned to be forwarded to Lord Stirling, I cannot hear anything further of, which I can't account for."

With winter at hand, "our men lay out in huts made of boards in a rough manner," the major reported. More than a few members of the regiment hadn't reported to camp. "There no doubt are many of our soldiers straggling in Philadelphia," He suggested that recruiting officers "should collect and march the stragglers to the regiment."

Sunday, December 8

Militia 'went hurry-scurry' in rain, snow

On Sunday the 8th, the soldiers in Sergeant Young's militia detachment crossed the Delaware into Pennsylvania, "marched about a mile from the shore and pitched our tents." They devoted much of Monday the 9th to improving their shelter. They "got boards to floor our tents and cover them so as to keep out rain, and to make it as comfortable as we could in this advance season of the year." They also fashioned "a ... common house ... to cook in and to sit in bad weather. We were pleased with the works of our hands; it was just dark when we had finished."

Suddenly, Young said, "orders came (that) we must decamp, for Howe's people designed to cross at Dunk('s) Ferry," about twenty miles below Trenton. "All the three battalions obeyed the order. At it we went hurry-scurry, almost head-over-heels. Set out at dark; hadn't marched far before it began to rain and snow. Wind at northeast. Very cold."

The night march proved to be a miserable one, "it being dark and the roads bad." Young himself had charge of the wagon at the rear of his brigade. "Some of the front wagons often stalled, which halted all behind them for near twenty times, which made our march very disagreeable," the sergeant wrote.

Taken at the site of Dunk's Ferry on the New Jersey side of the Delaware River, the photograph looks across the river to Pennsylvania.

It was 3 A.M. on Tuesday, December 10, when the soldiers arrived at the ferry over Neshaminy Creek in lower Bucks County, "all as wet as rain could make us and cold to numbness," he said. Troops that had arrived before Young's unit had crowded into the ferry house. Although there was a fire blazing in the fireplace, "we could not get to the fire on account of the numbers in the house," Young said.

The Pennsylvania side of Dunk's Ferry was about a mile or so beyond Neshaminy Creek, and Young's company didn't arrive there until about 10 A.M.

Even as Young's company had moved upriver on Thursday, December 5th, to take up positions along the Delaware, substantial numbers of retreating Continental soldiers began arriving in Philadelphia. City residents were shocked to see how poorly they were dressed. Marshall and three of his friends—Paul Fooks, Thomas Smith, and Leonard Keassler—went door-to-door, "a begging for old clothes for the naked soldiers coming from camp."

Detail of map dating to mid-1770s shows Trenton, Bordentown, Burlington, Bristol, and, in lower left, Dunk's Ferry. The map is dedicated to "Thomas Penn and Richard Penn, Esquires, true and absolute Proprietaries and Governors of the Province of Pennsylvania."

Philadelphia's panic intensified on Sunday, December 8. As Marshall wrote tersely: "News brought of General Howe's intentions of bringing his army by land through the Jerseys to this city, martial law declared, and General (Israel) Putnam constituted chief ruler in this Province."

Monday, December 9, became a day of "hurry and confusion," Marshall said. "All shops ordered to be shut; the militia to march into the Jerseys. . . . News that General Howe is on his march."

The events of Tuesday, December 10, were even more stressful. "Our people in confusion, of all ranks, sending all their goods out of town into the country," Marshall noted. "News brought that our army had sent their heavy baggage from Trenton (to) this side of the river; the enemy advancing in great order, and was at Brunswick. . . . Great numbers of sick soldiers arriving into the town."

New Brunswick was forty miles southeast of Manhattan and sixty miles northeast of Philadelphia.

Wednesday, December 11

'Our Congress leaves . . . for Baltimore'

Confidence in the Continental Army's ability to stop the British advance had dropped so low by Wednesday, December 11, that "our Congress leaves this city for Baltimore. The militia going out fast for Trenton. Streets full of wagons, going out with goods," Marshall wrote.

By Thursday the 12th, Philadelphians learned that "Howe's Light Horse were at Princeton, and that General Washington with all his troops had come over (the) Delaware." Marshall's diary entry for Friday, December 13, notes that Howe's advance troops had arrived in Trenton, about thirty miles upriver and part of his force had come even closer—to Burlington, only twenty miles to the northeast.

If these events unnerved Philadelphians who supported the Revolution, Loyalists found them somewhat reassuring. Many of Philadelphia's Loyalists were Quakers. "The Friends here moved but little of their goods, as they seem to be satisfied that if General Howe should take this city, as many here imagined that he would, their goods and property would be safe," Marshall said. In contrast, residents who feared a British occupation were "still sending their goods" out of town.

General William Howe

The next day—Saturday the 14th—brought "alarming and fresh accounts of Howe's near approach," Marshall said. These reports sent even more "people hurrying out of town."

On Sunday the 15th came news "that Howe's troops had attempted to cross our river at several places and several times, but (were) always repulsed, so that he could not effect it. Our troops increasing and in high spirits."

Wednesday, December 11

'Keep a good lookout for spies'

By Wednesday, December 11, Washington realized that the British were shifting more and more troops to the southwest, putting them ever closer to within striking distance of Philadelphia. To counter this, he saw an urgent need to strengthen the guards at the river crossings. These included Dunk's Ferry, suddenly important because it was only seventeen miles up the Delaware from Philadelphia. "From the movement of the enemy downwards, I think it highly necessary that the post at Dunk's Ferry should be guarded," Washington said.

Writing from the Falls of the Delaware opposite Trenton, Washington informed Colonel Cadwalader, who had come up from Philadelphia with three militia battalions, to post his brigade in and around Bristol, a Bucks County village on the Delaware about twenty miles north of Philadelphia, with another regiment several miles downstream at Dunk's Ferry. "Establish the necessary guards—and throw up some little redoubts at Dunk's Ferry," the commander ordered.

Cadwalader was also to fortify the passes along the Neshaminy Creek, which flowed into the Delaware from the west about five miles below Bristol. "Pay particular attention to Dunk's Ferry as it's not improbable something may

John Cadwalader

be attempted there," Washington said. "Spare no pains or expense to get intelligence of the enemy's motions and intentions."

The general ordered Cadwalader to act at once. "I, therefore, desire that one of the battalions of your brigade may immediately march, and take post at that place," Washington said. "The other two battalions should be under orders to march at a moment's warning."

Although General Howe and other top British officers had by now pulled back to New Brunswick and other places in East Jersey, Washington had no intention of relaxing his vigilance. Hessians remained at Trenton, Bordentown, and Burlington, which was only three miles upriver from Dunk's Ferry. "If the enemy attempt a landing on this side, you give them all the opposition in your power," he told Cadwalader. "Should they land between Trenton Falls and

Bordentown Ferry—or anywhere above Bristol—and you find your force quite unequal to their force, give them what opposition you can . . . without hazarding the loss of your brigade. Keep a good guard over such boats as are not scuttled or rendered unfit for use. Keep a good lookout for spies. Endeavor to magnify your numbers as much as possible."

Should the British "rout you from your post, you are to repair to the strong ground near Germantown unless you have orders from me or some other general officer to the contrary," Washington said.

Germantown was a village about nine miles north of Philadelphia and about sixteen miles southwest of Dunk's Ferry.

Friday, the 13th

'Where is the guard? Why don't they fire?'

Born and raised in Maryland, James Wilkinson spent 1773 to 1775 in Philadelphia as a medical student. He had begun to practice medicine in northern Maryland when the British attacked American troops outside of Boston on June 17, 1775. Decades later, Wilkinson recalled, "I abandoned my profession forever, and at my own expense repaired to the camp before Boston, in September, and as a volunteer, joined the rifle corps under the gallant Colonel William Thompson of Pennsylvania."

Superior officers recognized the youth's abilities. By December 1776, Wilkinson had attained the rank of brigade major and had become an aide to Major General Horatio Gates. On December 2, Gates left Albany, New York, with seven regiments and headed south to rendezvous with Washington in New Jersey. Ten days later, Gates was marching across northern New Jersey. As he approached Sussex County Courthouse (present-day Newton), he sent Wilkinson on ahead to locate Washington with a request "for your Excellency's orders in respect to the route you would have me take."

Riding off, Wilkinson soon learned that Washington had crossed the Delaware into Pennsylvania and that "the boats had been removed from the ferries, and that I should find some difficulty in getting across the Delaware." Informed by an officer he met on the road that Major General Charles Lee was at Morristown, Wilkinson changed course and, riding all night, sought out Lee. Well before dawn on Friday, December 13, he found the general accompanied by a small guard and bedded down at White's Tavern in the remote village of Basking Ridge. Lee's army, Wilkinson noted, was two miles away.

In his memoirs, Wilkinson said that General Lee didn't rise until around 8 o'clock, and "wasted the morning in altercation with certain militia corps who were of his command." The day proceeded at a leisurely pace, and "we did not sit down to breakfast before 10 o'clock."

Since Lee was one of the Continental Army's top-ranking officers, Wilkinson gave him the letter that Gates had written to Washington. He read it, and after breakfast, "General Lee was engaged in answering General Gates's letter."

Wilkinson said that Lee was just finishing his reply. "I had risen from the table, and was looking out of an end window, down a lane about one hundred yards in length ... when I discovered a party of British dragoons turn a corner of the avenue at a full charge."

The riders soon surrounded the inn. Lee exclaimed, "Where is the guard? Damn the guard! Why don't they fire?"

The raiders had caught the guard without their weapons, and the dragoons chased them down.

When Wilkinson saw that Lee had just signed the letter to Gates, "I caught up my pistols, which lay on the table, thrust the letter he had been writing into my pocket, and passed into a room at the opposite end of the house."

A British officer, Captain Thomas Harris, said Lee didn't give up immediately. "After firing one or two shots from the house, he came out and entreated our troops to spare his life," Harris said.

Wilkinson said he was still inside the inn when he heard a British officer shout, "If the general does not surrender in five minutes, I will set fire to the house."

Lee soon surrendered. Wilkinson watched as "Lee, mounted on my horse, which stood ready at the door, was hurried off in triumph, bareheaded, in his slippers and blanket coat, his collar open, and his shirt very much soiled from several days use."

The dragoons were interested only in capturing Lee. Once they had him in hand, they rode off, leaving Wilkinson and the other American soldiers scot-free.

As Wilkinson noted, "if General Lee had not abandoned caution for convenience and taken quarters two miles from his army, on his exposed flank, he would have been safe."

Lee's second-in-command was General John Sullivan. It was Sullivan's December 13 dispatch, which an express rider rushed to the American camp in Bucks County, that finally gave Washington the hard information that he had sought about General Lee for several weeks.

"It gives me the most pungent pain," Sullivan wrote, "to inform your Excellency of the sad stroke America must feel in the loss of General Lee, who was this morning taken by the enemy near Veal Town (present-day Bernardsville.) . . . By some fatality, he was induced to go . . . nearer the enemy by three miles than we were. Some Tories doubtless gave information, and this morning seventy of the light horse surrounded the house, and . . . he was made a prisoner."

Although White's Tavern was less than forty-five miles from Washington's camp, it took two days for Sullivan's express rider to reach Washington with Sullivan's letter, which also reported that Sullivan was bringing Lee's division to Pennsylvania.

General Sullivan required more than a week to march his troops across northern New Jersey.

"That division of the army, late under the command of General Lee, now General Sullivan, is just upon the point of joining us," Washington reported to Hancock on Friday, December 20. "A strange kind of fatality has attended it! They had orders on the 17th of November to join, now more than a month!"

Washington added, "General Gates with four eastern regiments are also near at hand . . .."

General Horatio Gates

William S. Stryker reported in his 1898 classic *History of the Battles of Trenton and Princeton* that Sullivan marched into camp on the 20th with two thousand soldiers. Gates had brought his force two hundred and twenty miles from Albany. When he reached Washington, he had "but five hundred effective men, and they had suffered greatly in a severe snowstorm which had detained them on the road through Sussex County, New Jersey, in the valley between the Walpack and the Kittatinny ridges," Stryker said.

Saturday, December 14

Cadwalader sends spies into New Jersey

On Saturday, December 14, Washington ordered his brigadier generals to defend the Delaware's west bank at all costs. To accomplish this, they needed to identify "the most probable crossing places, have those well watched, and direct the regiments or companies most convenient to repair as they can be formed, immediately to the point of attack, and give the enemy all the opposition they possibly can."

"Everything," the general said, ". . . depends upon the defense at the water's edge. . . . one brigade is to support another without loss of time, or waiting orders from me."

"As your numbers are rather small," Washington wanted his officers to fool enemy observers on the Jersey side. "Now and then, to the best advantage, an appearance might be made with those you have as if fresh troops were coming in."

The generals should also "cast about to find . . . some person" willing to cross into New Jersey and spy on the enemy. Such a spy should determine "if any preparations are making to cross the river, whether any boats are building, and where." Washington noted pointedly, "If possible, get some person into Trenton and let him be satisfied if any boats are building at that place and on Crosswicks Creek," which flows into the Delaware about eight miles below Trenton at Bordentown.

The spy should find out "whether any (enemy troops) are coming across land from Brunswick. Whether any great collection of horses are made, and for what purpose."

The commander told the generals that "expense must not be spared in procuring such Intelligence, and will readily be paid by me." He also urged caution in recruiting spies: "We are in a neighborhood of very disaffected people. Equal care should, therefore, be taken that . . . these persons do not . . . betray us."

Writing from Bristol on Sunday, December 15, Colonel Cadwalader advised Washington that he had sent several spies into New Jersey, and that they had returned with news of Hessian troop movements: "One of the men sent yesterday morning to Mount Holly . . . conversed with a man well known for his attachment to our cause, who informed him that six hundred (Hessians) lay last night at the Black Horse, about nine miles from Burlington." Situated due east of Burlington, Black Horse is the present-day Columbus, New Jersey.

Cadwalader gave Washington a detailed account of his spy's report: "He saw them on their march in the following order. The advanced party of two hundred near the Black Horse; two hundred at Mansfield Meeting; two hundred at the Rising Sun, or Square. This line extended about three miles, but the whole were to march to the Black Horse. They had five brass field pieces."

Cadwalader added that as his spy made his way back to Pennsylvania, "he came through Burlington and was there informed that the troops seen at Black Horse were the advance party of about two thousand Hessians."

The colonel was sufficiently pleased by the quality of the information his spies had brought back that he dispatched another agent to New Jersey, headed this time toward Bordentown. He explained, "General Ewing informed me yesterday that upwards of two thousand Hessians were seen going into Bordentown." Cadwalader said that he had asked his spy to confirm this information. "The person sent over today is a very intelligent, spirited officer in the Jersey regulars," he said.

Around this time, word reached Washington's headquarters in the Bucks County village of Newtown that "Cornwallis is going to England to tell the King that the rebellion is about over," an anonymous staff officer wrote in his journal on Sunday, December 22. Newtown is six miles west of Trenton.

General Howe, meanwhile, had decided to spend the winter in Manhattan. "Howe is going to have a good time in New York attending dinner parties," the officer wrote.

Saturday, December 14

Delaware troops march on blistered feet

Downriver in Delaware, "a general dismay seemed spread over the country," reported Captain Thomas Rodney of Delaware's Kent County Militia.

On Saturday, December 14, Rodney's militia company—known as the Dover Light Infantry—departed Dover, bound for Philadelphia nearly eighty miles to the north and, ultimately, for Washington's encampment at present-day Washington Crossing some hundred and ten miles north of Wilmington. The company's thirty-five infantry troops marched "at 3 o'clock in the afternoon . . . the ground being covered with snow several inches deep." Rodney himself set out from Dover the next morning and quickly caught up. En route, they learned that three other Delaware units had already struck out for the Continental Army's camp.

On Monday the 16th, "we reached Wilmington, where we encamped all night," the captain wrote. The men "were fitted out with knapsacks, canteens, etcetera."

At the town of Christiana Bridge, which took its name from the bridge over the Christiana River at Wilmington, "we saw the road full of the citizens of Philadelphia who had fled with their families and effects, expecting the British army would be there in a few days."

These refugees included Thomas McKean, a Philadelphia lawyer who represented Delaware in the Continental Congress, "and several other congressmen on their way from Philadelphia to Baltimore." McKean told Rodney, whose brother Caesar also represented Delaware in the Congress, "that everything was very gloomy and doubtful and that the chief hope that remained was that General Lee, who was on the mountains in the rear of the enemy, would be able to effect some lucky stroke that would prevent the enemy's crossing the Delaware."

But McKean also emphasized that "if nothing of this sort happened, Congress would be obliged to authorize the commander-in-chief to obtain the best terms that could be had from the enemy."

Neither McKean nor Rodney knew it, but news had just reached Philadelphia that "General Lee was taken prisoner through treachery," as Marshall reported in his diary for December 16.

Wednesday, December 18

Philadelphia 'made a horrid appearance'

Rodney's company marched into Philadelphia on Wednesday, December 18. The men endured the five-day trek "in good health and spirits, but some have blistered feet," the captain wrote.

The soldiers were surprised, even startled, by conditions in the city itself. "It made a horrid appearance. More than half the houses appeared deserted, and the families that remained were shut up in their houses, and nobody appeared in the streets," Rodney said.

The militiamen were also surprised to learn that "there was no military of any kind in the city, only General (Israel) Putnam, who was there to give orders to any militia that might come in. I had a sentinel placed at the general's door, and others to guard the city that night." A major general in the Continental Army, Putnam had served with distinction in the Battle of Bunker Hill near Boston in 1775.

Rodney then went to a coffee house, "but there was no one there." A man named Bradford served Rodney "a bowl of punch and some biscuit, and I sat in a box alone. I asked Bradford what was the reason no one appeared, and he said that they expected the British in every moment and were afraid."

The night passed without incident, and on the morning of Thursday, December 19, Rodney decided to visit Philadelphia relatives of his wife, whom he described as "Quakers and very great Tories." "I went to see Joshua Fisher's family," he wrote. His in-laws surprised him. "They seemed glad to see me, were all extremely cheerful, said that the contest would soon be over now, that the British would be in town in a day or two, and invited me to sup at Thomas Fisher's that evening."

Rodney accepted the invitation and found his Loyalist in-laws welcoming and cordial. "They were all particularly friendly to me," he wrote. "After supper, several kinds of good wine were placed on the table, and I drank, what was usual with me, about three glasses of Madeira."

When the conversation inevitably turned to the war, they advised him, "that now was a favorable time to relinquish all further opposition."

"They informed me, I believe very truly," Rodney wrote, "of the situation of the British and American armies; told me General Lee was certainly taken prisoner; that there was no prospect that America could make any further exertions. That it was, therefore, in vain for me to attempt anything more."

The Fishers said, "that they expected the British in town in a few days," and promised to do what they could to keep Rodney from harm. They told him that "they would engage that neither myself nor my brother nor any of my friends should be injured and that I might expect on the contrary any favor I would ask."

This was an extraordinary promise. Not only was Rodney's brother Caesar a general in the Delaware State Militia, but he was also a member of the Continental Congress and a signer of the Declaration of Independence.

Rodney replied: "I answered them by pointing out those circumstances that were still favorable to America and concluded by assuring them that I should not change my determination, that I knew my business and should not return until the British were beaten."

The Fishers "treated this as levity and concluded that I was an obstinate man," the captain said. The conversation continued for a long time, "and then as it was now pretty late (Rodney) parted from them and went to my quarters."

Events in Philadelphia continued to gather momentum. Marshall wrote on Wednesday, December 18, that he saw "great numbers of the country militia coming in to go to join General Washington's army." There was also "news that our army intended to cross at Trenton into the Jerseys." On Thursday the 19th, "a large number of our troops left this city to join some in the Jerseys, in order to pursue and attack a number of Hessian troops, who, it's said, had come as far as Moorestown . . . in the Jerseys." Moorestown was a mere fifteen miles east of Philadelphia.

It was Saturday, December 21, when Captain Rodney and the Delaware militiamen left Philadelphia, headed for Washington's camp more than thirty miles upriver. "A continual snow fell last night and cleared up with rain and sleet, and the weather is very cold," the captain wrote in his journal. "Today, in getting ready to march, I went through the city and found it almost deserted by the inhabitants, and looking as if it had been plundered." He added, ". . . scarcely a chair can be had at a public house to sit down in, or a meal of victuals to be had." In sharp contrast, and "to our great joy, we saw the streets full of militia and hundreds pouring in every hour."

Saturday, December 21

Griffin's grand diversion lures Hessians

In charge of Philadelphia's defense, General Israel Putnam in mid-December sent his deputy adjutant, Colonel Samuel Griffin, across the Delaware River and into southern New Jersey with a small strike force.

Griffin's detachment included two companies of Virginia troops, an assortment of Pennsylvania soldiers, and, if Loyalist Joseph Galloway's account is to be believed, "boys picked up in Philadelphia and the (New Jersey) counties of Gloucester and Salem."

When militiamen in southern New Jersey learned Griffin had entered the region, they quickly rallied to support him, swelling his force to about five hundred men.

General Howe had posted British soldiers inland at Princeton, and Hessians along the Delaware at Trenton, Bordentown, and Burlington. At first, Griffin was well south of these positions, but he soon worked his way north toward Burlington and Bordentown.

By Saturday, December 21, Griffin had reached Mount Holly, a village about twenty-six miles east of Philadelphia, but only seven miles east of Burlington and thirteen miles south of Bordentown. Colonel Carl von Donop commanded the Hessians at both locations.

As Griffin approached Donop's region, a Burlington County Loyalist named Barzella Haines was sent to Mount Holly to spy on Griffin. Haines subsequently reported that he arrived in Mount Holly on Saturday, December 21, "in the night and lodged in the rebel camp there." According to British intelligence documents, the spy saw "only two field pieces, which he thinks were three pounders as he perceived them at the church." Since "all the troops were drawn up in his view," Haines easily assessed the strength of Griffin's force: "He walked round them and thinks there were not above eight hundred, near one half boys and all of them militia, a very few Pennsylvanians excepted.... He knew a great many of them, who came from Gloucester, Egg Harbor, Penns Neck, and Cohansey," all places in southern New Jersey.

Also on December 21, Captain Friedrich Heinrich Loray advised Colonel Johann Rall, the Hessian commander at Trenton, that the Hessians probably didn't have anything to fear from Griffin. "My patrols went as far as Springfield (a village about sixteen miles south of Trenton), and I heard that there are seven hundred men at Mount Holly, but it is not likely that they will undertake anything. I really believe that the whole party is nothing but a rebel patrol," Loray said.

On Sunday, December 22, Griffin's men skirmished with British and German troops at a bridge near Black Horse (present-day Columbus, N.J.). According to the Hessian commander, two Hessians and two Scots were wounded. Donop himself "went... to Black Horse. I found the enemy had all except a few patrols moved out no farther than the meeting house this side of Mount Holly." He posted two battalions at Black Horse and a third battalion between Black Horse and Bordentown. Then he returned to Bordentown. At around 3 o'clock, Donop heard alarm guns fired by these troops, "and I . . . returned instantly to Black Horse."

When the colonel reached Black Horse, "I found my men all under arms because as soon as I had left four or five hundred rebels had attacked the picket at Rancocas bridge but effected nothing but the withdrawal of the twelve Scottish soldiers and their sergeant. Captain von Eshwege who was quartered with his company in a house near(by) came to their assistance, and a picket of grenadiers that was stationed just beyond him, and the rebels did not move a step further."

Other sources place this skirmish at a bridge over Assiscunk Creek near Black Horse and state that it occurred on Monday, December 23. The span had a picturesque name, Petticoat Bridge, and the fighting there is sometimes referred to as the Battle of Petticoat Bridge. The Assiscunk and Rancocas creeks are tributaries of the Delaware River and flow from east to west. In 1776, the village of Mount Holly was along the North Branch of Rancocas Creek.

Saturday, December 21

Lee's capture made 'everything gloomy'

It took Rodney's company more than a day to march the twenty miles to General Cadwalader's camp at Bristol. Washington's headquarters were located another twelve miles up the Delaware. By 2 P.M. on Saturday, December 21, "we reached Bristol, where the Philadelphia volunteers are encamped," Rodney wrote.

The Delaware men quickly learned that no lodging was available in the town, and the quartermaster there sent them about two miles from Bristol to the residences of William Coxe and Andrew and Sarah Allen on the banks of the Neshaminy Creek.

Andrew Allen's father, William Allen, had been a former chief justice of the Pennsylvania Supreme Court and a former mayor of Philadelphia. Allen himself had been an organizer of a Philadelphia militia company in 1774 and a Pennsylvania delegate to the Second Continental Congress in 1775. But when other representatives began calling for independence, Allen had balked, and by late 1776 had become a Loyalist. In early December, when Generals Howe and Cornwallis led their army into west New Jersey, Allen and two of his brothers, William and John, left Pennsylvania, crossed into New Jersey, and joined them.

Rodney reported that half of his men obtained lodging at the nearby home of William Coxe, a prosperous Philadelphia merchant who was a Loyalist. The others were quartered at the Allen residence. "Mrs. Allen . . . prepared a room for me and requested that I would stay at her house to prevent her being insulted as her husband and brothers had fled to the enemy, and she, therefore, had been insulted some days before," Rodney said. He added, "Both families treat myself and the whole company with the greatest kindness and politeness."

Cadwalader summoned Rodney for a meeting in Bristol on the evening of Sunday, December 22.

"I waited on him, and he asked me what number of men I had brought," Rodney said. "I told him thirty-five. He asked me if that was all. I told him it was, and I thought they were enough, and asked him how many he had there, and how many General Washington had left."

The colonel replied that he "had had twelve hundred, but many had gone off one way or another.... He supposed there was still eight hundred left." Cadwalader said that he thought General Washington still had about fifteen hundred men. Soldiers who had belonged to General Lee's army had recently arrived in the American camp. Lee's recent capture "had damped the spirit of the army very much, and everything looked very gloomy," Cadwalader said.

The colonel emphasized that the Americans needed more soldiers, but "I replied that there was no occasion for more men, that there was enough for any enterprise, and the measure ought not to be delayed a moment on that account, for now was a favorable time, and I had not the least doubt of success, but if men were wanting, there would soon be enough, for the roads were full from Virginia and Pittsburgh to Philadelphia," Rodney said.

Rodney explained that he had been ordered to lead the Kent County militia to Washington's camp, but Cadwalader said that "the commander-in-chief had directed him to stop all militia there, and if I would stay he would send an express to him."

Rodney replied that if Washington "said I might stay, then I would do so. So General Cadwalader sent an express immediately to the general, and I returned to my quarters at Mrs. Allen's."

Washington's headquarters at Newtown was only about twelve miles away, and the express rider completed the round-trip journey that night with Washington's orders that Rodney and the Delaware men should stay at Cadwalader's post.

Also, Cadwalader "informed me that he wanted us to join a party of Philadelphia militia that night to make a tour into the Jersey and harass the enemy, and asked me if the men were fit to go."

"I told him that a number of them were, and would willingly go," but others were still worn out from their hundred-mile march, and the captain wanted them exempted from the raid. When Cadwalader realized "they had marched so far, he would not permit any of us to go," Rodney said.

Cadwalader paraded the other troops assigned to the raid at 2 A.M. on Monday, December 23, but canceled the mission altogether when he learned that Colonel Samuel Griffin wasn't prepared to join him. In mid-December, Griffin had taken with two companies of Virginia troops into South Jersey, where Jersey militiamen had joined him and swollen his force to about five hundred men.

On December 22, Colonel Joseph Reed advised Washington that "Colonel Griffin has advanced up the Jerseys with six hundred men as far as Mount Holly within seven miles of their headquarters at the Black Horse." Griffin had also written to Cadwalader at Bristol, requesting "two pieces of artillery and two hundred or three hundred volunteers as he expected an attack very soon."

Reed, who was one of Washington's aides, crossed the Delaware, visited Griffin in Mount Holly, and reported that he "found Colonel Griffin in bad Health and was informed that his force was too weak to be depended on either in numbers or discipline. That all he expected was to make a diversion."

Colonel Joseph Reed

Sunday, December 22

'As soon as the Delaware freezes'

By late December, the opposing armies had settled in on opposite sides of the Delaware. As an officer on Washington's staff wrote in his diary on Sunday, December 22, the Americans had twenty-five hundred men under Generals Sullivan and Greene at McConkey's Ferry (present-day Washington Crossing. Pa.) A short distance below Trenton, Brigadier General James Ewing had two thousand men, and a little more than ten miles downriver, "General Cadwalader and General Putnam are at Bristol . . . with as many more."

Intelligence arriving at Washington's headquarters in Newtown indicated General James Grant with a few hundred English troops at Princeton, Colonel Rall with fifteen hundred Hessians at Trenton, and Count von Donop with two thousand Hessians at Bordentown, along the river about eight miles below Trenton.

Americans, soldiers as well as civilians, were feeling downright glum. "A scout just in says that General Howe has issued a proclamation, offering pardon to everybody in New Jersey who will lay down their arms and take the oath of allegiance," the staff officer said.

Soldiers on the Delaware's Pennsylvania side felt secure if the river didn't freeze.

"I rode along the river yesterday morning and could see the Hessians in Trenton," the staff officer said. "It is a pretty village, containing about a hundred and thirty houses and a Presbyterian meeting-house. A stone bridge spans the Assinpink Creek on the road leading south to Bordentown. There are apple orchards and gardens."

The Hessians were a colorful lot. As Stryker reported, infantrymen belonging to one regiment wore bright red coats while members of another had uniforms of dark blue. Soldiers in the third regiment had plain black uniforms. The artillerymen wore blue coats with crimson lapels and white border, and the riflemen dressed in green with lapels of crimson.

For their part, the Hessians kept watching the river. "The Delaware, which is here extremely rapid . . . , separates us and the rebels," a German officer wrote on Friday, December 13. ". . . As soon as the Delaware freezes, we may march over and attack Philadelphia, which is about thirty miles distant."

The Hessian had formed a poor opinion of both the village and its residents. "This town consists of about one hundred houses, of which many are mean and little," he wrote. As the Hessians had approached, many residents had fled and had taken their belongings and furniture with them. He said that he and a friend had obtained lodging "in a fine house belonging to a merchant, and we have empty rooms enough. Some of the servants of the inhabitants remain here. Last evening, I gave one a box on the ear for his sauciness. I bid him bring me a candle, and he replied, if I wanted candles, I should have brought them with me. I was furnished with a candle, but nothing else."

The officer noted that the Americans continually harassed the Hessians. "We are obliged to be constantly on our guard," he said.

On Tuesday, December 3, for instance, a captain of the grenadiers was shot crossing a bridge by "a rebel who had concealed himself under the bridge." On Monday, December 16, "the rebels came over the river in boats, but effected nothing." On Wednesday the 18th, "seventy rebels came over the water, and we were obliged to turn out. But they only carried off a family who went willingly, with three cows and some furniture." The next day, "a troop of rebels" badly wounded an English soldier on horseback near Maidenhead (present-day Lawrenceville) about seven miles due north of Trenton. Two days later, "a horseman was shot dead."

The Hessian's entry for Tuesday, December 24, reported that "the enemy actually attacked our grenadiers last night, but without success," although three men were wounded.

"We have not slept one night in peace since we came to this place. The troops have lain on their arms every night, but they can endure it no longer," the officer said.

Although Colonel von Donop, the Hessian commander at Bordentown, "wrote to us . . . , desiring us to be on our guard, for that he was certain of being attacked," the soldiers at Trenton didn't take the warning too seriously. They were aware of the raggedy conditions of many Continentals. "That men who . . . have neither coat, shoe nor stocking, nor scarce anything else to cover their bodies, and who for a long time past have not received one farthing of pay, should dare to attack regular troops in the open country . . . is not to be supposed," the officer wrote in an entry dated Tuesday, December 24.

Monday, December 23

Donop entertains a 'beautiful widow'

On the morning of Monday, December 23, Colonel von Donop took a substantial force of Hessians to Mount Holly, where Griffin's militia troops had occupied a hilltop near a church and an ironworks. "I met a few hundred men at the meeting house, but after firing a few shots, they ran away, and the whole party took the road to Moorestown," about nine miles to the southwest. "I had no wounded or dead men, but the rebels had three caused by my artillery fire," the colonel said.

Although the Hessian colonel sent one of his three battalions back to quarters at Mansfield Square near Bordentown, he had the two other battalions remain at Mount Holly "to gather food and forage for the stores at Bordentown." Donop himself remained in Mount Holly, where "the colonel, who was extremely devoted to the fair sex, had found in his quarters the exceedingly beautiful widow of a doctor," according to Captain Johann Ewald, the officer of an elite Hessian rifle company.

Ewald said that Donop's entire corps "took up quarters in the town." The captain described Mount Holly as an "excellent trading place ... inhabited by many wealthy people. Since the majority had fled and the buildings had been abandoned, almost the whole town was plundered.

And because large stocks of wine were found there, the entire garrison was drunk by evening.... The grenadiers were bringing in so much wine that the majority of *jagers* became merry toward midnight, and I had great trouble to keep them together."

The *jagers* were Hessians who carried rifled guns with hexagonal barrels, had short swords at their sides for hand-to-hand fighting, and wore green coats.

Tuesday, December 24, was the day before Christmas. On Tuesday night, Washington sent Reed on a fast trip to Philadelphia to confer with General Putnam. Reed reported that "he found Colonel Griffin had returned very ill, (and) that the two companies of Virginians had also returned, leaving their two small pieces of iron cannon and a few militia" in New Jersey.

Wednesday, December 25

Flints, ammunition have been distributed

In the late afternoon, the American soldiers began retrieving the boats stashed along the Pennsylvania side of the Delaware—behind Malta and other islands. Most were Durham boats, flat-bottomed vessels that came to a point at each end. Capable of carrying heavy cargo in shallow water, these boats were sixty feet long. They were plentiful along the river between Easton and Philadelphia. The ironworks at Durham, a village south of Easton, used them to ship iron nearly sixty miles downstream to Philadelphia. Millers, farmers, and other commercial operators used them to haul various commodities up and down the Delaware.

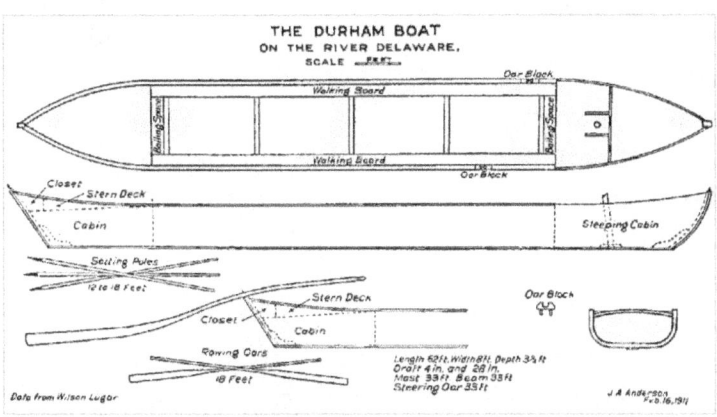

Fully loaded, a Durham boat sixty feet long and eight feet wide "would carry, downstream, one hundred and fifty barrels of flour or about six hundred bushels of shelled corn," wrote J.A. Anderson in his 1912 book, *Navigation on the Upper Delaware*. The ordinary boat carried cargo weighing between two and five tons. From gunwale to keel plank, the sides of the boat measured forty-two inches—waist high for a man six feet tall. To power a boat, crewmen used oars eighteen feet long and poles twelve to eighteen feet long. To steer, the captain used a steering oar that was thirty-three feet long. Most of these boats lacked seats for passengers.

Washington understood the strategic value of these boats. Back on Sunday, December 1, he told William Livingston, the governor of New Jersey, that it was urgent to move all boats—and "particularly the Durham boats"—along the Delaware to the Pennsylvania side. The Durham boats were especially valuable because "one such boat would transport a regiment of men," Washington said.

Now that it was Christmas, the general intended to employ these boats to transport his army across the Delaware. "Colonel Glover's fishermen from Marblehead, Massachusetts, are to manage the boats just as they did in the retreat from Long Island," an officer on Washington's staff wrote in his diary.

Earlier in the day, the Continentals had cooked rations for three days for each man. By late afternoon, "new flints and ammunition have been distributed," the staff officer wrote.

Just before sunset, the Pennsylvania riflemen who were camped at Thompson's Mill received marching orders, which Sergeant McMichael called "glad news." He

Colonel John Glover

elaborated: at sundown, "we with undaunted fortitude paraded at camp near Coryell's Ferry" and then marched south along the Delaware for about five miles.

By 6 o'clock, the army began gathering at McConkey's Ferry. "It is fearfully cold and raw, and a snow-storm setting in," the staff officer wrote. "The wind is northeast and beats in the faces of the men. It will be a terrible night for the soldiers who have no shoes. Some of them have tied old rags around their feet. Others are barefoot."

Sergeant McMichael reported later that he and the men in his battalion "crossed to New Jersey at McConkey's Ferry at 9 o'clock P.M." He added, "after a hesitation of some few hours at the ferry, we proceeded to Trenton, the weather being uncommonly inclement."

The crossing took much longer than Washington had anticipated. "Glover's men have had a hard time to force the boats through the floating ice with the snow drifting

A John Warner Barber (1798–1885) woodcut showing Durham boats carrying soldiers in the Continental Army across the Delaware River in 1776.

in their faces," the staff officer wrote. "We are three hours behind the set time,"

Colonel Henry Knox, responsible for the army's eighteen field pieces, said that getting the guns across to New Jersey provided the Massachusetts sailors "with almost infinite difficulty." In a letter written two days later, Knox said, "The floating ice in the river made the labor almost incredible. However, perseverance accomplished what at first seemed impossible."

Midnight, December 25

Ewing found the Delaware too icy to cross

At about midnight, General Ewing took his soldiers to the Pennsylvania side of the Delaware, a short distance below Trenton. He found the river too icy to risk an attempt to cross it.

"We were to have crossed the river at Trenton under General Ewing but could not do it in consequence of the drift ice," recalled Daniel Parkinson, a private in a Pennsylvania regiment.

"We turned out under arms at midnight, but not being able to cross the river, we slept upon our arms until daybreak," the seventy-eight-year-old Parkinson said when he applied for a military pension in 1832. In the morning, the river remained too ice-choked for boats to take the soldiers over. They remained on the Pennsylvania shore and listened to "the fire of our army commencing."

According to Washington's staff officer, Ewing's mission had been "to cross (the Delaware) and seize the bridge crossing the Assunpink." The bridge was part of the road linking Trenton and Bordentown. This was important strategically because Washington planned to attack Trenton from the other side of the town. If they took the bridge, Ewing's men would block any Hessians who attempted to flee to Bordentown. Also, the Americans would be in a position to prevent any rescue party that Donop might send up from Bordentown.

Ewing's division consisted of five Pennsylvania regiments from Chester, Cumberland, Lancaster, and York counties; a regiment of Bucks County militia; and detachments of New Jersey militiamen from Hunterdon and Middlesex counties. These units contained more than a thousand commissioned officers and enlisted men, but on Christmas night, Ewing's force was significantly smaller. Most soldiers weren't available for duty that night. The Cumberland County regiment commanded by Colonel Frederick Watts, for example, had a total of a hundred and eighty-nine men, officers, as well as rank-and-file troops, on its roster. Still, only seventy-five were ready and able to make the crossing. The others—a hundred and fourteen men—were either absent, sick, or on extra duty, Stryker reported.

Indeed, only two hundred and seventy-seven of the seven hundred twenty-five Continental soldiers in Ewing's command were fit for duty, and the militia troops assigned to his command numbered between three hundred and five hundred, according to Stryker.

Thursday, December 26

Ice impedes the transport of cannons, men

Washington had wanted all his men and artillery on the New Jersey shore by midnight so they could reach Trenton by 5 A.M. on Thursday, December 26. "But the quantity of ice," Washington wrote, ". . . impeded the passage of boats so much that it was three o'clock before the artillery could all be got over, and near four, before the troops took up their line of march."

With the nine-mile march finally underway, Washington divided his force in two, then accompanied General Nathanael Greene, who took the upper road through Pennington. General Sullivan marched along the road that followed the river.

When Sullivan saw that many of his soldiers were unable to shield their firearms from the rain and snow and that their muskets had become so wet that they were unfit for service, he sent a messenger to Washington for guidance. One of Washington's staff officers overheard Washington's reply: "Tell General Sullivan to use the bayonet. I am resolved to take Trenton."

The storm slowed the march considerably. "The night was sleety, and the roads so slippery that it was daybreak when we were two miles from Trenton," an officer said in

American soldiers marching to Trenton.

a letter published in The Pennsylvania Evening Post on Saturday, December 28.

Colonel Knox reported that the two columns approached Trenton "at the same time, about half an hour after daylight . . . The storm continued with great violence, but was in our backs, and consequently in the faces of our enemy."

The Hessians at Trenton—"in all about fourteen hundred men in and around the town," according to Stryker—consisted of three regiments of infantry, as well as a detachment of artillery, and fifty Hessian riflemen who were called *yagers* or *jagers*. There were also twenty light dragoons belonging to the Sixteenth British regiment.

The Continentals encountered the first of these troops at outposts a short distance from the village. "About half a mile from the town was an advanced guard on each road, consisting of a captain's guard," Knox wrote. "These we forced, and entered the town."

As they approached Trenton along the Pennington Road, Washington and Greene had been out of contact with Sullivan for quite some time and didn't know whether he was also nearing the village. On the outskirts of town, their column came to a house where a picket guard was stationed—"about twenty men under Captain Altenbrockum," the staff officer wrote. The Hessians "came running out of the house. The captain flourished his sword and tried to form his men. Some of them fired at us. Others ran toward the village. The next moment we heard drums beat and a bugle sound, and then from the west came the boom of a cannon. General Washington's face lighted up instantly, for he knew that it was one of Sullivan's guns."

As Washington later told John Hancock, "The outguards made but small opposition, though, for their numbers, they behaved very well, keeping up a constant retreating fire from behind houses. We presently saw their main body formed, but from their motions, they seemed undetermined how to act."

The fighting quickly escalated. The Hessians "endeavored to form in streets," Knox said. But the Continentals had already placed their cannon and howitzers at the heads of these streets. "These, in the twinkling of an eye, cleared the streets," he said.

Many Hessians took shelter behind houses, but "the musketry soon dislodged them," Knox said. "Finally, they were driven through the town into an open plain beyond. Here they formed in an instant. . . . The poor fellows, after they were formed on the plain, saw themselves completely surrounded." These soldiers soon surrendered.

American soldiers firing a cannnon.

In the town, "We could see a great commotion down toward the meeting-house, men running here and there, officers swinging their swords, artillerymen harnessing their horses," the staff officer said. "Captain Forrest unlimbered his guns. (General) Washington gave the order to advance, and we rushed on to the junction of King and Queen streets. Forrest wheeled six of his cannon into position to sweep both streets."

Events happened swiftly. Washington said later that from a vantage point on the northern side of town, he watched as a large number of Hessians "attempted to file off by a road on their right leading to Princeton, but perceiving their Intention, I threw a body of troops in their way which immediately checked them."

The staff officer added more details. "The riflemen under Colonel Hand and Scott's and Lawson's battalions went upon the run through the fields on the left to gain possession of the Princeton road," he said.

Back in the village itself, German artillerymen were organizing to oppose the Americans. "The Hessians were just ready to open fire with two of their cannon when Captain (William) Washington and Lieutenant (James) Monroe with their men rushed forward and captured them," the officer reported.

As Monroe wrote later in his 1830 autobiography, "The (Hessian) drums were beat to arms, and two cannon were placed in the main street to bear on the head of our column as it entered. Captain Washington rushed forward, attacked, and put the troops around the cannon to flight and took possession of them. Washington presently "received a severe wound and was taken from the field," wrote Monroe, who took command. As the eighteen-year-old lieutenant advanced at the head of Washington's men, he "was shot down by a musket ball which passed through his breast and shoulder." Both men survived.

The Hessian commander, Colonel Johann Rall, had been sound asleep when the attack began. Roused, he dressed quickly, left his headquarters at the Trenton residence of wealthy businessman Stacy Potts, mounted his horse, and raced toward the fighting.

"We saw Rall come riding up the street from his headquarters," the staff officer wrote. "We could hear him shouting in Dutch (German), 'My brave soldiers, advance!' His men were frightened and confused, for our men were firing upon them from fences and houses, and they were falling fast. Instead of advancing, they ran into an apple orchard. The officers tried to rally them, but our men kept advancing and picking off the officers."

Someone shot Colonel Rall, and he "tumbled from his horse, and his soldiers threw down their guns and gave themselves up as prisoners," the staff officer said.

As the Pennsylvania Evening Post reported in its December 28 edition: "The enemy, consisting of about fifteen hundred Hessians... formed and made some smart fires from the musketry and six fieldpieces, but our people pressed from every quarter, and drove them from their cannon."

Quoting "a letter from an officer of distinction," the newspaper said that the Hessians "retreated towards a field behind a piece of wood up the creek from Trenton and formed in two bodies..." Soon after this, General Washington, accompanied by the letter writer, "came in full view of them from the back of the wood... (and) an officer informed him that the party had grounded their arms and surrendered."

Early in the battle, as the Continentals entered Trenton, the British cavalrymen made a fast exit. "A party of their light horse... made off on our first appearance," the Evening Post reported, quoting the officer's letter.

As the Continentals advanced on the village from the north, they couldn't control traffic on the stone bridge over Assunpink Creek, which ran along the south side of Trenton. "About six hundred (Hessians) run off upon the Bordentown Road the moment the attack began," reported Tench Tilghman, another member of Washington's staff, in a letter written the next day.

As the fighting progressed, General Sullivan "sent a portion of his troops under (General Arthur) St. Clair to seize the bridge and cut off the retreat of the Hessians toward Bordentown," the staff officer wrote. "Sullivan's men shot the artillery horses and captured two cannon..."

The battle eventually ended as the Hessians, seeing themselves surrounded, "agreed to lay down their arms," Washington later told Hancock. "The number that submitted in this manner was twenty-three officers and eight hundred and eighty-six men. Colonel Rall, the commanding officer, and seven others were found wounded in the town. I don't exactly know how many they had killed, but I fancy not above twenty or thirty, as they never made any regular stand. Our loss is very trifling indeed, only two officers and one or two privates wounded."

Before leaving Trenton, Washington visited the wounded Hessian colonel. "I have just been with General

Hessian prisoners were taken to Newtown where they were held at the Presbyterian Church. They were later sent to Philadelphia.

Washington and Greene to see Rall," the staff officer wrote in his diary. "He will not live through the night. He asked that his men might be kindly treated. Washington promised that he would see they were well cared for."

Rall died on the evening of Friday, December 27.

Tench Tilghman wrote, "Our loss is only Captain Washington and his lieutenant (Monroe) slightly wounded, and two privates killed, and two wounded."

As Sergeant McMichael reported, "We returned that day to the ferry at McConkey's, transported the prisoners to Newtown, and after a dreadful fatigue we arrived at camp (at Thompson's Mill), so having obtained a comfortable lodging I found Morpheus (an ancient god of sleep) . . . had possession of me, and so I betook myself to my silent rest."

Wednesday, December 25

Cadwalader's men cross at Dunk's Ferry

Downriver at Bristol, "We had about eighteen hundred rank-and-file" soldiers ready to make the crossing, General John Cadwalader reported.

Returning to Newtown from Philadelphia, Colonel Joseph Reed, Washington's adjutant general, stopped at Bristol late on Christmas Day. "At this place lay the Pennsylvania Militia, chiefly composed of the city battalions, very well provided for the field, and also about five hundred Rhode Island troops . . . under the command of Colonel (Daniel) Hitchcock, without shoes or blankets and otherwise in wretched plight . . . ," Reed said later. According to Reed, the force at Bristol amounted to about fifteen hundred men commanded by Cadwalader, who had been "appointed a militia brigadier general a few days before."

In the late afternoon, the newly minted general rode to the river bank and inspected the spot where he had planned to cross, but "the river was so full of ice that it was impossible to pass above Bristol, where I intended, and therefore concluded to make an attempt at Dunk's Ferry," Cadwalader said afterward. The ferry was about five miles below Bristol.

As Washington had done upriver, Cadwalader had stored boats along the river on the Bristol side. Three days earlier, a British spy—identified only as "Captain Losbiniere"—had visited Cadwalader's posts at Bristol and the Neshaminy Ferry and counted not only troops but boats and cannons as well. He reported that at Bristol, Cadwalader had "not more than" eight hundred or nine hundred men, and five cannons: three iron four-pounders and two brass six-pounders. He also saw seven flat-bottom boats and two ferry boats. Each boat could carry about fifty men. He said there weren't any entrenchments or redoubts. At Neshaminy Ferry, Losbiniere noted, "there were two companies . . . with some boats."

"As soon as it was dark, I sent down all the boats I could muster, and marched down about 8 o'clock," Cadwalader said. "I embarked a few men to line the river and prevent any person escaping to give intelligence to the enemy, and these were followed by a part of the first battalion of militia, then two field pieces."

Sergeant Young's company didn't receive orders to march until nightfall when the militia soldiers were told "to hold ourselves ready to move with two days provision." They took part in what Young described as "a grand parade at seven this evening." Two hours later, they set out for Dunk's Ferry.

As Reed recounted later, "About sunset the boats moved down (the Delaware) from Bristol, and at dark, the troops began their march, the light infantry and militia in front and the Continental troops in the rear." Reed said that "when they arrived at the ferry, the light infantry pushed over in the first boats and landed on the opposite shore in a few minutes, the weather being fine though cold."

The commanding officers had wanted "to keep the troops from kindling any fires on the shores before they embarked," but the night became so cold, "we were obliged to take our chance of giving the enemy the alarm."

Captain Rodney's Delaware company crossed over in the first boats leaving Pennsylvania with orders "to cover the landing of the brigade."

"The river was . . . very full of floating ice, and the wind was blowing very hard," Rodney wrote. ". . . The night was very dark and cold, and we had great difficulty in crossing." He added that "when we reached the Jersey shore, we were obliged to land on the ice, a hundred and fifty yards from the shore. . . . We advanced about two hundred yards from the shore and formed in four columns of double files."

Rodney reported that "about six hundred of the light troops got over, but the boats with the artillery were carried away in the ice and could not be got over."

At some point, Cadwalader crossed over to New Jersey "to see if it was practicable to land" the cannons, and "upon examination found it was impossible, the ice being very thick." By this time, a second battalion had landed. Cadwalader said that he conferred with his field officers, and all concluded "that it would not be proper to proceed without cannon."

Cadwalader ordered the men to return to Pennsylvania. As Rodney wrote later, the order to go back angered the men. "After waiting about three hours, we were informed that . . . Cadwalader . . . had given up the expedition, and that the troops that were over were ordered back," Rodney said. "This greatly irritated the troops that had crossed the river, and they proposed making the attack without . . . the artillery."

A spirited discussion took place, with the cooler heads contending "that if General Washington should be unsuccessful and we also, the Cause would be lost, but if our force remained intact, it would still keep up the spirit of America. Therefore, this course was abandoned," Rodney wrote.

The captain said later that the return trip to the Pennsylvania shore took three hours, "by which time the wind blew very hard, and there was much rain and sleet, and . . . so much floating ice in the river that we had the greatest difficulty to get over again, and some of our men did not get over that night."

Colonel Reed offered details that were similar to Rodney's account. The colonel said that he and several field officers crossed over on the heels of the first boats. "To their great surprise . . . they found the ice had drifted in such great quantities upon the Jersey shore that it was absolutely impossible to land the artillery," Reed said. These officers managed to get their horses off the boat and onto land "with such difficulty as excluded all hope of debarking the field pieces."

Cadwalader eventually decided to call off the mission, but the order came so late that "nearly all" of the troops had been transported to New Jersey, Reed said. He added: "They accordingly began to re-embark with great reluctance. By this time, the ice began to drive with such force and in such quantities as threatened many boats with absolute destruction. To add to the difficulty, about daybreak, there came on a most violent storm of rain, hail, and snow intermixed."

Captain Rodney added, "As soon as I reached the Pennsylvania shore, I received orders to march to our quarters, where I arrived a little before daylight very wet and cold."

Sergeant Young reported that the wind accompanying the rain and snow came out of the east northeast and was "very cold. Our men came home very wet and cold." The Philadelphia troops spent Thursday, December 26, in their quarters, "drying their clothes," the sergeant said.

As his troops returned to Bristol, Cadwalader promptly wrote a letter to General Washington in which he described and justified his decision to call off his mission. It contained an intriguing line: "I imagine the badness of the night must have prevented you from passing as you intended."

Although the distance separating Washington's headquarters at Newtown and Cadwalader's force at Bristol was a mere twelve miles, it was night by the time Cadwalader and his troops received news of Washington's success at Trenton.

"Heard last night that General Washington had defeated Howe's men at Trenton," Sergeant Young wrote in his diary on Friday, December 27. "Had it confirmed this morning."

"In the evening, we heard of General Washington's success at Trenton and that he had captured nine hundred Hessians," Captain Rodney wrote. He noted that General Ewing's expedition at Trenton "has also failed, and I am inclined to think that General Washington meant these only as feints."

In a Friday, December 27, letter to John Hancock, Washington described his victory at Trenton and stated the consequences of Cadwalader and Ewing failing to reach their objectives. "General Ewing," Washington wrote, "was to have crossed before day at Trenton Ferry, and taken possession of the (Assunpink Creek) bridge leading out of town, but the quantity of ice was so great, that though he did everything in his power to effect it, he could not get over. This difficulty also hindered General Cadwalader from crossing with the Pennsylvania militia from Bristol."

Cadwalader "got part of his foot (soldiers) over, but finding it impossible to embark his artillery, he was obliged to desist," Washington said, adding, "I am fully confident that could the troops under Generals Ewing and Cadwalader have passed the river, I should have been able with their assistance to have driven the enemy from all their posts below Trenton."

Thursday, December 26

Col. von Donop leaves Mount Holly abruptly

Donop's occupation of Mount Holly came to a sudden end on the afternoon of the 26th. That's when another officer "reported to me that he had heard by a messenger that the rebels had surprised the Rall brigade this morning at Trenton," Donop wrote. Initial reports reaching Mount Holly placed the size of Washington's army at "ten to twelve thousand strong" and said erroneously that "a large part of the rebels had turned to Princeton."

When the Hessian colonel learned the extent of Rall's defeat, he moved his corps as quickly as possible to defensive positions closer to Princeton, thirty miles to the north. "I did not think it advisable for me to remain any longer in so dangerous a situation, surrounded by the enemy and cut off from all communication with Princeton," the colonel wrote to General Knyphausen, his superior officer.

The Hessian officer also disclosed that he had been "compelled to leave about twenty sick and wounded at Bordentown, with a stock of provisions and forage. Some of the men were not able to be carried, and the wagons were too scarce to carry the rations, which will, therefore I fear, fall into the hands of the rebels."

He added that his force had absorbed nearly three hundred Hessians, all members of the Rall brigade, who had managed to escape capture at Trenton. He had organized them into "a force of two hundred and ninety-two men, including the command at the drawbridge of one captain, three officers, and one hundred men." This bridge spanned Crosswicks Creek on the road between Trenton and the New Jersey village of Allentown, about twelve miles east of Trenton.

By Friday the 27th, Donop had reached Allentown, about sixteen miles south of Princeton. The colonel also reported, among other things, a "shortage of ammunition." He added, "This place is so situated that I can push through from here or, in one day if necessary, resume my former position."

The colonel made no mention of the doctor's widow at Mount Holly. He did, however, disclose that communications he had received on Christmas Day hadn't alarmed him. "There was nothing in Colonel Rall's reports, and, more especially, in the communications from General (James) Grant (at Princeton) to fear at Trenton," Donop said. "The following morning, I regret to say, proved the contrary."

Donop told General Knyphausen that Colonel Rall deserved the blame for the defeat. "All agree . . . that if Colonel Rall with his brigade had retreated over the (Assunpink Creek) bridge and then destroyed it, he could have saved his command instead of fighting for an hour against such heavy odds."

Friday, December 27

Cadwalader crosses the Delaware again

Important news sometimes traveled very slowly between Washington's headquarters at Newtown and Cadwalader's camp at Bristol. The militia general had learned of the American victory at Trenton on the evening of Thursday, December 26, the same day as the battle, but didn't find out until mid-day Friday, December 27, that the Continental soldiers, accompanied by their Hessian prisoners, had returned to Pennsylvania.

Mistakenly thinking that Washington had remained in New Jersey, Cadwalader and his officers decided to cross the Delaware on Friday morning, march to Bordentown twelve miles upriver, and dislodge the Hessians stationed there. After leaving Bordentown, Cadwalader's men would then move north about eight miles and join Washington at Trenton.

Cadwalader and his officers had decided on this course of action on Thursday, December 26. "We have determined to pass over to the neck of land a little above Bristol at six in the morning," Cadwalader said in the second letter he sent to Washington that day.

Cadwalader also reported that "General Putnam . . . was to go over from Philadelphia today (Thursday the 26th) with five hundred men, which number added to the four hundred Jersey militia which Colonel Griffin left there would make a formidable body."

Still unaware of Washington's return to Pennsylvania, Cadwalader led his force over the Delaware on the morning of the Friday the 27th "and landed about fifteen hundred men about two miles above Bristol."

The Delaware remained awash with ice, and this crossing was far from easy. Sergeant Young, the Philadelphia wagoner, reported that the men in his company rose before daybreak and prepared to move out. For Young, this meant loading baggage in his wagon. The sergeant went along when the battalion moved out, and "marched to Bristol. There unloaded it aboard a flat-bottomed boat, and with much difficulty got over on account of the ice and by the good providence of God."

Washington didn't learn of Cadwalader's plan until the operation was well underway. "I was just now favored with your two letters of the 25th and 26th instant," the commander wrote. He asked Cadwalader to put his plan on hold and explained that he wanted to drive the rest of the Hessians from the region but hadn't yet decided how to do this. "If we could happily beat up the rest of their quarters bordering on and near the river, it would be attended with the most valuable consequences," Washington said. "I have called a meeting of the general officers to consult of what measures shall be next pursued and would recommend that you and General Putnam should defer your intended operations till you hear from me."

Washington's missive reached Cadwalader too late. Only "after a considerable number were landed" in New Jersey did Cadwalader learn that Washington's army was back in Bucks County. "This defeated the scheme of joining your army," he told the commander-in-chief later. "We were much embarrassed which way to proceed. I thought it most prudent to retreat, but Colonel Reed was of opinion that we might safely proceed to Burlington and recommended it warmly least it should have a bad effect on the militia who were twice disappointed."

Cadwalader reported that making "the landing in open daylight must have alarmed the enemy, and we might have been cut off by all their force collected to this place." But that didn't happen. "We had intelligence immediately afterwards that the enemy had left the Black Horse and Mount Holly," Cadwalader said. "Upon this, we determined to proceed to Burlington."

Cadwalader's decision to remain in New Jersey and then march to Burlington had been much more complicated than his letter to Washington suggests. Writing long after the war, Colonel Reed added many details.

To begin with, a shipment of clothing had arrived from Philadelphia for Colonel Daniel Hitchcock's Rhode Island troops on the night of Thursday the 26th. Distributing these clothes on the morning of Friday the 27th delayed their departure for New Jersey. By 1 P.M., "the militia had all landed (in New Jersey), and the Rhode Island troops were about to embark" when news arrived "that General Washington had recrossed the river with his prisoners," Reed reported. "This unexpected circumstance threw us into the greater perplexity and occasioned a variety of opinions."

Some officers contended that with the main Continental army back in Pennsylvania, "there were no troops to support us" if Cadwalader remained in New Jersey and "that Count (von) Donop was equal if not superior in numbers and might soon march back from Mount Holly,"

Reed said. These officers contended that should the Hessians stop Cadwalader's advance, "a retreat over the river would be impracticable and the consequences fatal."

"Colonel Hitchcock of the Continentals was strongly of this sentiment and urged the return not only on account of the state of his troops, but the hazard of continuing on the enemy's shore with such a force and such raw troops," Reed said.

On the other hand, withdrawing from New Jersey at this point would discourage many Pennsylvania militiamen, whom Reed characterized as "taken from their families and kept out a long time without action." These troops had already "began to grow uneasy," and making them return to Pennsylvania without fighting might have triggered "a general desertion," Reed said.

"Long and pretty warm debates ensued," the colonel said. "Of those who were against returning, some were for proceeding to Mount Holly to attack the Hessians . . . others to march on to Bordentown, which might be expected to be weakly provided with troops in Donop's absence." At length, a compromise emerged "that the troops should proceed to Burlington where they could wait for further advice and proceed to Bordentown or Mount Holly as the intelligence might direct or if necessary, embark and return to Bristol."

"About 3 o'clock, the whole army got in motion towards Burlington," Captain Rodney reported. "The order of march was, first Colonel (Timothy) Matlack's rifle battalion on the right and left in single file, advanced about two hundred yards before the infantry. Next the light infantry in four columns of double files. Next the artillery, and then the main column following in platoons, flanked at two hundred yards by single files in the woods."

Colonel Reed told what happened as Cadwalader's force headed toward Burlington. "We then pushed on towards the enemy's outposts, which were about four miles from Burlington," Reed said. The soldiers "halted at a small distance from the place where their pickets usually" were posted. They moved ahead cautiously, and, "seeing no smoke or appearance of men advanced to it and found it evacuated."

The Hessians had fled. The Americans interrogated nearby residents who told them "that the guards in this neighborhood had gone off precipitately the preceding evening," Reed said.

Reed, who had left Cadwalader and ridden north to Bordentown, added that as he approached Bordentown, he saw that "almost every house on the road had a red rag nailed upon the door," which, with the Hessians suddenly gone, "the inhabitants were busily pulling down."

The men with Cadwalader continued their way to Burlington, and they remained on the road long after dark. "In this order, we reached Burlington about 9 o'clock, and took possession of the town," Captain Rodney said.

There weren't any Hessians at Burlington, either. "We found that the enemy had fled from there and all the adjacent parts in great precipitation," Rodney said. "The general therefore gave orders that our light troops should march at 4 o'clock tomorrow morning. The troops were quartered in houses, but it being now 11 o'clock they had but about four hours to sleep. This town is opposite Bristol on the River Delaware, and most of the houses are brick, but as it was dark when I went in and we left it before day, I can give no description of it."

Saturday, December 28

Cadwalader advances on Bordentown

General Cadwalader hadn't yet learned that the Hessians had fled when his advance troops left Burlington at 4 A.M. on Saturday, December 28, and marched along the Great Road to Bordentown, which was about ten miles upriver. "Along the road, we saw many Hessian posts at bridges and crossroads," Captain Rodney reported. "They were chiefly made with rails and covered with straw, all deserted. The whole country, as we passed, appeared one scene of devastation and ruin. Neither hay, straw, grain, or any livestock or poultry to be seen."

It took the soldiers a full five hours to reach their objective. According to Rodney, "We got to within half a mile of Bordentown about 9 o'clock, and made a halt just at the foot of a bridge, where we heard that the enemy had deserted the town and were about five miles off, but were disposed to return, and that some of their light horse were expected every minute."

The Americans took up positions in a cornfield adjacent to Bordentown "and set posts on all the roads," Rodney said, "but after waiting thus about an hour were informed that the enemy were flying with all speed. We then marched into the town in several detachments, and took possession of a large quantity of stores which the enemy had left, then went into quarters and refreshed ourselves, and in about two hours, the main body of the army came up."

Rodney described the damage the Hessians had done to the village: "This little town is pleasantly situated on the River Delaware ... above Burlington. The houses are chiefly brick, and several of them large, elegant, and neat, but they all look like barns and stables, full of hay, straw, dirt, and nastiness, and everything valuable about them destroyed and carried off, and all the inhabitants fled. Here had been the headquarters of Lord or Count Donop, one of the Hessian generals, but it looked more like the headquarters of a swineherd. Mr. Borden's house had some hundred pounds worth of goods and valuable furniture ruined and broken to pieces."

As Cadwalader's men hunted for the Germans in Colonel von Donop's command, the Hessian prisoners captured at Trenton were being moved away from the front lines.

"Hessian prisoners are expected from Newtown, Bucks County, in this city tomorrow," Christopher Marshal, the retired Philadelphia druggist, noted in his diary on Saturday, December 28. But the POWs didn't arrive until Monday. "Near eleven, the Hessian prisoners, to the amount of nine hundred, arrived in this city, and made a poor, despicable appearance," Marshall said. The influx of German prisoners continued on Wednesday. "More Hessians and their officers, with many of their wounded, (were) brought to town this day and evening," Marshall noted.

By Sunday, December 29, General Cadwalader's force had moved several miles north of Bordentown to the bridge over Crosswicks Creek, about four miles south of Trenton.

"At this place, the woods are quite alive with men," Sergeant Young wrote in his journal. "All are illuminated with large fires."

Monday, December 30

'Orders were given for our party to charge'

Washington and the Continental Army returned to Trenton on Monday, December 30, aware that the British had a sizeable force at Princeton about twelve miles to the northeast. In need of reliable intelligence, Washington had a special mission for Reed, a shopkeeper's son who had grown up in Trenton and retained a working knowledge of the region's roads and villages.

The general had him take a patrol out "to reconnoiter the advanced posts" toward Princeton.

In his memoirs, Reed said that he headed northeast toward Princeton, "accompanied . . . by six horseman, members of the Philadelphia city troop." They traveled for about nine miles until they were three miles from Princeton. Along the way, they attempted to hire some of the country people to travel into the town and gather information about the British and the Hessians, but "no rewards would tempt the inhabitants . . . to go into Princeton on this errand."

Reed's patrol pressed closer to the town. "As we were passing slowly on, almost within view of the town, a British soldier was observed passing from a barn to the dwelling-house without arms." The Philadelphians suspected that the man was a marauder, and "two of our party were sent to bring him in." When they spotted two other British soldiers, "orders were given for our whole party to charge."

They quickly surrounded the house. Surprised, "twelve British soldiers, equipped as dragoons and well-armed, their pieces loaded, and having the advantage of the house, surrendered to seven horsemen, six of whom had never before seen an enemy," Reed said. "The sergeant only escaped."

Thursday, January 2, 1777

British return for the 2nd Battle of Trenton

Despite the American victory at Trenton, many Continental soldiers left the army when their enlistments expired on Wednesday, January 1.

General Thomas Mifflin had additional troops at Bordentown. The combined force of Cadwalader's column and Mifflin's troops totaled about thirty-six hundred men. "They were ordered to join us at Trenton, which they did by a night march" on Wednesday, January 1, Reed said.

Sergeant Young said that the order came through somewhere around midnight and 1 A.M. on Thursday, January 2, the temperature had risen, and traveling conditions that night were deplorable.

"It rained when we set out," said Young, who drove a baggage wagon at the rear of his brigade. He reported that "on account of the thaw, the road was very muddy and deep . . . Its being night, I could not see my way. The moon gave some light, but it being on my back, I could not see so as to get the best road." The sergeant added that although the troops left Crosswicks between midnight and 1 A.M. and "we had but eight miles to go, it was 9 o'clock before we reached Trenton" in the morning.

Now that the Continental Army, its ranks depleted, had returned to Trenton, Washington's troops had their backs to the Delaware. The Americans expected the British to attack, and Lord Cornwallis didn't disappoint. On Thursday the 2nd, "the enemy began to advance upon us, and after some skirmishing, the head of their column reached Trenton about 4 o'clock," Washington reported later to John Hancock. ". . . They attempted to pass Assunpink Creek, which runs through Trenton at different places, but finding the fords guarded, halted, and kindled their fires."

The Americans "were drawn up on the other side of the creek. In this situation, we remained till dark, cannonading the enemy and receiving the fire of their fieldpieces, which did us but little damage," Washington said.

In his journal, Sergeant McMichael of the Pennsylvania Rifle Regiment added other details: When word of the British advance reached the American camp at 10 A.M., "the drums immediately beat to arms. We were all paraded in the south side of the bridge. A thousand men under the command of Major General Sullivan were detached in front to bring on the attack, which they did and reached town at 5 P.M., but our artillery played so furiously, followed with our rifles that the enemy retreated out of town and encamped on an adjacent hill. We continued firing bombs till 7 o'clock . . . when we were ordered to rest."

Although he didn't take part in the fighting, Sergeant Young watched the combat. "I and my two sons saw the action," he wrote. "They cannonaded each other with that furiousness that it was Impossible to hold long. Our people retreated after exchanging the musketry for some time." The American moved with such "haste that the enemy took it for a flight. That drew them into the trap designed for them, which was a reserve of men and cannon that cut them in such a manner that put a stop to their advancing."

Young added, "As soon as night fell, our people lined the wood (and) made large fires. As soon as I could, I came to them with the wagon, with the provisions and blankets, and stayed with them till 12 o'clock, then loaded our wagon, (and) set out and joined my two sons whom I left in the wood with some of our men."

Seeing that the British outnumbered the Continentals, Washington opted to leave Trenton. "I ordered all our baggage to be removed silently to Burlington soon after dark, and at 12 o'clock, after renewing our fires and leaving guards at the bridge in Trenton and other passes on the same stream above, marched by a roundabout road to Princeton, where I knew they could not have much force left and might have stores," Washington said.

When the Continentals reached Princeton at sunrise, "only three British regiments and three troops of light horse (were) in it, two of which were on their march to Trenton," Washington said. "These three regiments . . . made a gallant resistance and in killed, wounded, and prisoners must have lost five hundred men. Upwards of one hundred of them were left dead in the field."

Sergeant McMichael endured the thick of the fighting. "General (Hugh) Mercer with a hundred Pennsylvania riflemen and twenty Virginians were detached in front to bring on the attack. The enemy then consisting of six hundred paraded in an open field in battle array. We boldly marched within twenty-five yards of them and then commenced the attack, which was very hot. We kept up an incessant fire till it came to pushing of bayonets, when we were ordered to retreat. Here General Mercer was mortally wounded . . .

Having retreated a small distance, we were reinforced when we immediately rallied, and with the utmost precipitation, we put them to the retreat. We killed sixty on the field, wounded seventy-five, and took two hundred and fifteen prisoners."

Thus, the Americans carried the day. Continentals killed during the fighting included General Mercer and several "other valuable officers who with about twenty-five or thirty privates were slain in the field," Washington told Hancock in a letter written two days later. "Our whole loss cannot be ascertained. . . . Many who were in pursuit of the enemy, who were chased three or four miles, are not yet come in."

The Americans had a close call in departing Princeton. "As soon as the enemy's main army heard our cannon at Princeton (and not 'til then), they discovered our maneuver and pushed after us with all speed," Captain Rodney reported.

About half a mile south of the battlefield, a bridge on the road to Trenton crossed a stream called Stony Brook. Washington had this bridge destroyed as a precaution, "and we had not been above an hour in possession of the town before the enemy's light horse and advanced parties attacked our party at the bridge, but our people by a very heavy fire kept the pass until our whole army left the town," Rodney said.

"We immediately evacuated Princeton proceeding through Kingston," Sergeant McMichael wrote. "We then steered right for Somerset Courthouse (present-day Millstone) where (we) arrived at 8 o'clock P.M."

Washington had considered advancing on New Brunswick, sixteen miles northeast of Princeton, but realized that his soldiers—"many of them having had no rest for two nights and a day"—were too exhausted to fight a third time. So, he led his army north along the Millstone River, a north-south stream that empties into the Raritan River about eight miles above New Brunswick. They spent the night of Friday, January 3, at "a little village called . . . Somerset Courthouse about fifteen miles from Princeton," Rodney wrote.

On Saturday the 4th, the army crossed the Raritan, then swung west and north, "and went to a place called Pluckemin, situated among the mountains of Jersey about ten miles from the last place," Rodney said. The soldiers set up camp in the westernmost of the Watchung Mountains and awaited "the coming up of nearly a thousand men who were not able through fatigue and hunger to keep up with the main body. . . ."

When Washington left Trenton two nights earlier, he had sent the baggage train to Burlington, about fifty miles south of Pluckemin. Consequently, the soldiers lacked much essential equipment. As Rodney said, "The army was obliged to encamp on the bleak (Watchung) mountains whose tops were covered with snow, without even blankets to cover them." As an officer, Rodney did a little better. "I had nothing to cover me here but my great coat, but luckily got into a house near the mountains where I fared very comfortably while we stayed here."

Rodney added, "Most of this army were militia, and they bore all this with a spirit becoming freemen and Americans."

Pluckemin, Sergeant McMichael wrote in his journal, "is situate on a valley bounded on the north and east by a

A John Warner Barber (1798–1885) woodcut showing the Continental Army winter encampment at Morristown, New Jersey, in January 1777.

chain of hills and on the south and west by a large plain which extends to (the) Delaware (River). Here we had the pleasure of encamping on the north side of a hill very well supplied with large stones which served us instead of pillows, and thus we passed two nights."

On Monday, January 6, "we left Pluckemin this morning and arrived at Morristown just before sunset," Captain Rodney said. The distance was roughly sixteen miles.

Sergeant McMichael's account provided a few more details. Also, on the 6th, the Pennsylvanians "marched from Pluckemin at 9 o'clock . . . and, steering for Morristown, we marched through Vealtown (present-day Bernardsville) and arrived at Morristown at 5 o'clock P.M. Here we encamped in the woods with snow on the ground, and as cold weather as I ever felt."

The next morning, "I . . . got to good quarters where I lived happily while we remained at Morristown with very agreeable inhabitants," the sergeant wrote.

Captain Rodney said that on the morning of Tuesday the 7th, "General Washington appointed my infantry regiment to be his own guard." He said that the general had made the choice "for the reason, I suppose, that they had distinguished themselves at Princeton and were the only regiment in the army that were in complete uniform, which was green faced with red."

Sergeant Young's Philadelphia teamsters were still at Burlington when orders reached them on the night of January 7 to depart for Morristown in the morning. "Got ready accordingly," Young wrote. ". . . Set out about 10. Marched to Trenton by night."

Young reported that it was noon on Thursday, January 9, when the convoy "passed through Pennytown (present-day Pennington) in company of one hundred fifty wagons, with a guard of three brigades, New Castle, Chester, and Cumberland. Halted at night about seventeen miles from Trenton." That night, the sergeant managed to sleep "at a German's house who had a stove in the room."

Two nights later, the sergeant reported that he "built a tent in the field. Got a good deal of hay. Very cold. Built a good fire. Sleep (sic) pretty well." On Sunday, January 12, their fifth and final day on the road, the teamsters "rose a good while before day," Young said. "Got breakfast by firelight." The convoy set out early and got to Morristown by noon.

The Pennsylvania riflemen left Morristown about three hours after the teamsters arrived and began the chore of setting up their winter camp. After five days, Sergeant

McMichael had come to dislike Morristown intensely. He described the village as "devoid of all beauty both in its form and situation."

To his relief, the regiment went to Chatham, about seven miles to the southeast on the Passaic River. McMichael obtained "very agreeable lodging where we found some beautiful young ladies, very amorous in their dispositions (and) all extremely fond of soldiers, but much more so of officers."

Captain Rodney remained at Morristown until Saturday, January 18, when he departed for Delaware. He left with a friend, Robert McGermot, after learning that his brother, General Caesar Rodney of the Delaware State Militia, had crossed into New Jersey with a large number of troops presumably bound for Morristown. "I determined to set off . . . to meet him," the captain wrote.

As they traveled, "we met sundry persons who had heard much cannonade towards New York." At Somerset Courthouse, along the Millstone River, they stopped at a tavern where a man said that he had spent the night in Elizabeth, a New Jersey town across from Staten Island, and "that a cannonade began at (New) York at 2 o'clock in the morning. The cannon fire had continued through the morning. The traveler said that he assumed the Americans were attacking New York, but beyond this didn't have any information.

Rodney said that when he and McGermot learned the tavern had run out of alcoholic beverages, they went to "the house of a man who had just obtained some rum and said he could make us a drink." After that, Rodney and McGermot "fell in with a gentleman from New York who invited us to lodge with him at a Dutch doctor's, just by, and we accepted the offer and were very agreeably entertained by the doctor."

The doctor, whom Rodney didn't identify, said that two British officers—one of whom was a Major Moyney—had boarded at the doctor's residence during early December. "They were both at his house when General Lee was brought there, a prisoner, by the Light Horse. . . . Major Moyney immediately ran out and kissed General Lee with tears in his eyes, and the general told him he never expected to see him in America," the physician said. "They all dined there together, and General Lee requested that the man who had betrayed him should be brought in, and when the general saw him, he abused him as a villain worthy the punishment of the most base and inhuman traitor."

The captain and his companion left Somerset Courthouse on the morning of Sunday, the 19th. They headed south toward Princeton, where they "rode out to see the battlefield and then went on towards Trenton." On the road, they met a "Mr. Tucker . . . who lives in Trenton. He informed me that my brother, with his brigade, was there, and I came on with him to Trenton, where I met my brother and his troops."

The captain spent nearly a week in Trenton with General Rodney. "When I came here, I had thoughts of going on home, but my brother insisted on my acting as brigade major for him, as he could not find a suitable person to perform that duty," the captain wrote.

The weather was bitter cold, and the Delaware River had frozen solid. Rodney noted that on Friday, January 24, "horses and wagons crossed the river on the ice."

The next day—Saturday, January 25—"about 10 o'clock I left Trenton and my brother, who was to march to Princeton next morning." By now, the Delaware was no longer frozen over. "The great rain that fell last night has broken it up, and this morning I crossed over in a boat, a little above the island, opposite the town," he wrote.

Rodney reached Philadelphia a few days later. Before leaving for Delaware, he made it a point to visit the Loyalist relatives of his wife, the Fishers. Five weeks earlier, these people had cheerfully informed Rodney that the rebellion would soon be crushed and that the British would presently occupy Philadelphia. They had offered to put in a good word for Rodney and his brother. When Rodney had disagreed with them, contending that events were "still favorable to America," his in-laws had dismissed him as "an obstinate man."

Since then, the Americans had won decisive victories at Trenton and Princeton, Philadelphia remained in the hands of the rebels, and General Howe had returned to Manhattan. These shifting fortunes of war had had a significant effect on the Fishers.

"They were all gloomy," Rodney said. "I reminded them that they were mistaken and that all was accomplished that I had foretold them, but they affected not to believe it, and I left them."

Captain Rodney made good time traveling the eighty miles between Philadelphia and Dover, Delaware, where he arrived on Tuesday, January 28. "I found all well," he wrote.

Monday, January 20, 1777

Militia wades icy river to fight British

A hundred and sixty militia soldiers belonging to the two Independent Companies of Westmoreland had left Wilkes-Barre on Wednesday, January 1, 1777, with orders to join General Washington's army in eastern Bucks County.

They followed an old Indian trail that took them out of the Wyoming Valley and into the mountains east of Wilkes-Barre. The path led eventually to a pass in the Blue Mountains called the Wind Gap and, below that, to a rough wagon road to Easton.

The march was far from a pleasant one. Heavy snow had fallen during the last week of December, followed by a hard rain on January 1. After that, there were several days of severe cold, which made the trail slick with ice.

These men considered themselves Connecticut troops. Part of Pennsylvania today, the Wyoming Valley was then part of Connecticut's newly created Westmoreland County. In 1662, King Charles II of England had given to Connecticut much of the territory that today is part of Northeast Pennsylvania. During the 1760s and early 1770s, more than a thousand Connecticut people migrated to the Susquehanna River's North Branch Valley and established farms and towns there. By mid-summer of 1776,

Westmoreland's population had grown to an estimated twenty-five hundred people, and in October 1776, Connecticut created Westmoreland County.

During the summer, the Wyoming men had organized two companies of soldiers intended to defend the valley. Few of these men had ever been under enemy fire. The soldiers in one company elected Robert Durkee as their captain; the men in the other company selected Samuel Ransom.

In mid-December, as the Continental Congress prepared to flee Philadelphia, it urged nearby states to send as their militias to reinforce the dwindling Continental Army. The Wyoming Valley companies were told "to join General Washington with all possible expedition." Washington was then in Bucks County along the Delaware. News of this reached Wilkes-Barre in late December, and the Westmoreland men departed on the 1st.

When the Wyoming troops reached Easton, "they learned that Washington had crossed the Delaware, had fought the battles of Trenton and Princeton . . . and was marching to Morristown, Morris County, New Jersey, to go into winter-quarters," reported author Oscar Harvey in his 1909 book, *A History of Wilkes-Barre, Luzerne County, Pennsylvania.*

By mid-January, most of Washington's Continentals were bivouacked in the mountains near Morristown, but the Wilkes-Barre troops found themselves stationed in an agricultural region south of the Raritan River at Somerset Courthouse, a strategic crossroads along the Millstone River.

Also posted at Somerset Courthouse (present-day Millstone) were four hundred troops of the New Jersey Militia. Indeed, there were more soldiers than villagers at the crossroads, and January brought periods of bitter cold. To keep themselves warm, the soldiers burned wood they took from fences that lined nearby farms.

The village was important because the east-west road that crossed here led to New Brunswick, about nine miles to the east. The British had many soldiers in that town.

To procure food, the British regularly sent small convoys of wagons into the countryside surrounding New Brunswick. The foragers simply showed up at a farm or gristmill and took livestock and whatever else they wanted.

The New Jersey militiamen, who knew the terrain intimately, often ambushed the British foragers. Consequently, English officers began sending out larger and larger squads of soldiers as escorts for the foraging parties.

Early on the morning of Monday, January 20, several hundred British regulars appeared at Van Nest's gristmill along the Millstone, about two miles north of Somerset Courthouse. They brought a convoy of more than forty horse-drawn wagons and several small cannons. They had amassed a substantial amount of livestock before reaching the mill, where they intended to confiscate a large quantity of flour the miller had planned to sell to the Continentals.

Nearby residents quickly spread the alarm, and soon the New Jerseyans and the Wyoming Valley men camped at Somerset Courthouse were hurrying toward the mill. General Philemon Dickinson, the New Jersey militia commander, took charge of the overall attack.

The New Jersey troops included Samuel Sutphen, a black slave owned by Casper Berger of Readington. Berger had purchased Samuel for the express purpose of sending him on militia duty as his substitute. In an 1834 application for a pension, Samuel described the action at the mill.

By the time the militia arrived, the British foragers "had plundered the mill of grain and flour and were on their way back to Brunswick but had not got out of the lane leading from the mill to the great road." The lane was a hundred yards long, and Samuel said it "was filled with four-horse teams. (Lieutenant) Davis ordered us to fire, and then we shot part of the first team, which stopped the whole drove. The drivers left their teams and run. A guard escorting the teams made their escape."

The fighting wasn't quite finished. "A party of Hessians, about one company, . . . was discovered secreted behind a hedge with some four or five fieldpieces. They fired on us and retreated." The New Jerseyans gave chase but eventually retreated. "The firing was principally across the river at the bridge," said Sutphen, who after the war had managed to purchase his freedom.

According to an eyewitness account printed in a Philadelphia newspaper:

> . . . To prevent our men from crossing, the enemy had placed three field pieces on a hill, about fifty yards from the bridge. When our men found it impossible to cross there, they went down the river, broke through the ice, waded across the river up to their middles, flanked the enemy, routed them, and took forty-three baggage wagons, a hundred and four horses, a hundred and fifteen head of cattle, and about sixty or seventy sheep. We lost four or five men. We took twelve prisoners . . .

The British fled to New Brunswick empty-handed, and the eyewitness, whose letter appeared in the Pennsylvania

Journal and Weekly Advertiser on January 29, provided more details:

> A man who came from Brunswick... says the enemy allow that they lost thirty-five or thirty-six men, but say the rebels lost three hundred. There were not more than four of our men crossed the river. The enemy report that they were attacked by three thousand of General Washington's troops there and were absolutely certain they were not militia; they were sure that no militia would fight in that way.

George Washington, in a January 22nd letter to Congress, happily reported that "General Dickinson's behavior reflects the highest honor upon him, for though his troops were all raw, he led them through the river, middle deep, and gave the enemy so severe a charge, that, although supported by three field pieces, they gave way and left their convoy."

If the Wyoming Valley men shared in the glory of the victory, they also suffered at least one casualty. As Charles Miner noted in his 1845 book, *History of Wyoming*, among those killed in action that day was "Porter, a gallant young fellow... cut down by a cannonball."

The Americans drove the wagons they had seized to Morristown. Sergeant Young, the Philadelphia teamster, watched the next day—Tuesday, January 21—when "the wagons taken yesterday came into town. The English horses taken are very poor..."

The comment formed part a lengthy entry that Young penned about day-to-day life at the Morristown encampment. "A fine warm afternoon," Young wrote. "I am about baking, have one oven now in, and another ready when the oven is heated."

Young noted that a young soldier in his company, John Towers, had become sick. That night, Young let the man "have my bed. I took my berth on the floor, which, being very open, let in plenty of wind, (which) made lying very uncomfortable. However, blessed be God, I am in good health."

Wednesday, January 22, became "a very fine day," the sergeant said in an entry piled high with non-sequiturs. He saw "a great concourse of people looking at the horses that our people took from the English.... Nothing new to-day. General Washington just riding by. May God long preserve his valuable life."

By Thursday the 23rd, Young's company had moved to the New Jersey hamlet of Chatham, southeast of Morristown. That night, he had slept on the floor of a house in the village. "The mistress of the house kindly let me and son lay in her room by the fire-side, for which favor I desire to be thankful," he wrote.

Young awoke early on the morning of Friday, January 24, and saw that it had snowed all night. "This morning, it turned to rain and very sloppy, it being the day we were to march home. Our company are uneasy to be home, but it being sloppy agree to stay a day or two longer in hopes it will be clear weather," he wrote.

John Towers, the young soldier, continued to be very sick. Another member of the company, a soldier named Forder, had also become seriously ill. Even so, when the company left Chatham headed for Philadelphia on Saturday, January 25, Forder and Towers went along. Apparently, the two men walked, because Young said their presence "somewhat retarded our march."

The soldiers passed through the village of Pluckemin, then forded the Lamington River, a small stream swollen by the rain and snow earlier in the week. They marched twenty-two miles and stopped just before sunset. "Our people are drying themselves after wading through Lamington," the sergeant said.

The men stayed at a house along the road. "The people where we quarter this night are somewhat shy of us," Young said. That was due to the conduct a few nights earlier of an officer and another soldier. "They behaved very rudely, insulted the people of the house, and other ways used them ill."

Young added, "We shall set out tomorrow for Coryell's Ferry to cross (the) Delaware, if the Lord permits." The Coryell family operated the ferry between present-day towns of Lambertville, New Jersey, and New Hope, Pennsylvania.

On Sunday, January 26, one of the ill men, Forder, suddenly began to hemorrhage. He "took such a bleeding at the nose that at his own request I left him at . . . a mill near the South Branch of the Raritan," Young said.

As the company proceeded to the Delaware, they passed a troop of Virginia light horse headed to Morristown.

On Monday, January 27, Young's men broke camp well before dawn and were on the road by 3 A.M. "With much fatigue got to Coryell's Ferry before 10," but traffic at the ferry was severely congested. Young said that five hours later, the Philadelphians remained on the New Jersey side "on account of the number of the Maryland militia that are coming over." It was after sunset when the company

A summertime view of the Delaware River between New Hope, Pennsylvania, and Lambertville, New Jersey. New Hope is on the far shore.

finally crossed into Pennsylvania and obtained quarters for the night with a "Mrs. Dobes at the ferry."

Sergeant Young spent the morning of Tuesday, January 28, "trying to get a light wagon with a cover to take Mr. Towers home, but as yet cannot get any." The sergeant did, however, succeed in finding someone who was leaving that day for Philadelphia, and the man agreed to locate the sick soldier's father and give him a message about his son, "which I don't expect he will get till tomorrow night."

A physician came in the late afternoon, examined the sick man, and said he had an advanced case of pleurisy, a disease of the lungs. "The doctor says he will do all he can for him and that if I take him in the wagon, his life will be in danger." Saying that Towers could stay with her, Mrs. Dobes arranged for a bed for him "in a warm room that has a good fireplace." Two soldiers in the company—John Smith and David Stentson—agreed to remain with him, and the doctor "sent some drops (for Towers) to take every two hours, forty at a time with another vial of liquid to take a spoonful every two hours."

Young's journal entry for the next day, Wednesday the 29th, began tersely: "Sat up with Mr. Towers till late last night to give him his physic, he being in a critical situation. Laid down and slept about four hours. Rose, loaded the wagon. Set out about 6. The road being rough we made but poor progress. Very poor accommodation on the road. About 10, it began to snow, which made our march very troublesome. Stopped often. Lay by the . . . side of Neshaminy (Creek) to rest our horses. Bought some bran and a loaf of bread. About 3 set out, and reached Abington about 6."

Abington is twenty miles southwest of New Hope and twelve miles north of Philadelphia.

The sergeant had an unpleasant surprise at Abington. At the end of a long, cold day, he halted the company "at a certain gentleman's house in comfortable expectation of quarters." He had hoped that his men could sleep in the kitchen and be able to stow their baggage indoors out of the weather. But the man, whom Young may have known, "resolutely refused, and used some unkind expressions." He also refused when Young asked for "the loan of tubs to feed our horses."

The sergeant explained that the company "intended to proceed to Philadelphia after our horses had fed and rested awhile. . . . I told him I only wanted to lay at his kitchen fire a few hours till the moon rose. It still snowed fast."

But the man rejected Young's request, "telling me there was a tavern a little further on, and a good deal more."

The man, whom Young didn't identify, went inside but came out again before the company had moved out. He had had a change of heart and told the sergeant that he would honor his request, "which, with some reluctance, I accepted." Young said that his men "at length put our baggage under his shed, our horses in his stable. Lay down by the kitchen fire. Very comfortable after eating some warm bread and milk."

On Wednesday, January 29, Sergeant Young "rose about 3 . . . Set out about 4. Reached home, and found my family all well, to my great satisfaction, about 10."

Selected Bibliography

Books

Duane, William, ed. *Extracts from the Diary of Christopher Marshall kept in Philadelphia and Lancaster during the American Revolution 1774–1781.* Albany: Joel Munsell, 1877.

Mazzagetti, Dominick. *Charles Lee: Self Before Country.* New Brunswick: Rutgers University Press, 2013.

Pennsylvania Archives. First series. Vol. IV. Edited by Samuel Hazard. Philadelphia: Joseph Severns & Co., 1853.

———. Vol. V. Edited by Samuel Hazard. Philadelphia: Joseph Severns & Co., 1853.

———. vol. VI. Edited by Samuel Hazard. Philadelphia: Joseph Severns & Co., 1853.

———. vol. VII. Edited by Samuel Hazard. Philadelphia: Joseph Severns & Co., 1853.

———. vol. VIII. Edited by Samuel Hazard. Philadelphia: Joseph Severns & Co., 1853.

———. vol. IX. Edited by Samuel Hazard. Philadelphia: Joseph Severns & Co., 1854.

———. vol. XII. Edited by Samuel Hazard. Philadelphia: Joseph Severns & Co., 1856.

The Pennsylvania Magazine of History and Biography. Vol. VIII. Philadelphia: The Historical Society of Pennsylvania, 1884.

The Pennsylvania Magazine of History and Biography. Vol. XXIX. Philadelphia: The Historical Society of Pennsylvania, 1905.

Reed, William B. *Life and Correspondence of Joseph Reed, military secretary of Washington, at Cambridge, adjutant-general of the Continental Army, member of the Congress of the United States, and president of the Executive Council of the State of Pennsylvania.* Philadelphia: Lindsay and Blakiston, 1847.

Rodney, Thomas. *Diary of Captain Thomas Rodney, 1776–1777.*

Wilmington: The Historical Society of Delaware, 1888.

Scheer, George F., and Hugh F. Rankin. *Rebels and Redcoats: The American Revolution Through the Eyes of Those That Fought and Lived It*. New York: The World Publishing Co. 1957.

Stryker, William S. *History of the Battles of Trenton and Princeton*. Boston and New York: Houghton, Mifflin and Company, 1898.

Wilkinson, James. *Memoirs of My Own Times*. Philadelphia: Abraham Small, 1816.

Internet resources:

Dictionary.com @ https://www.dictionary.com/
Google maps @ https://www.google.com/maps/
Internet Archive @ https://archive.org/

About the Author

John L. Moore of Northumberland is a writer and storyteller whose subjects deal with real people and actual events in Pennsylvania history.

Against the Ice is the fourth book in his Revolutionary Pennsylvania Series, which tells the stories of Pennsylvania and Pennsylvanians caught up in the American Revolutionary War. It is a companion to *Tories, Terror, and Tea* (2017), *Scorched Earth: General Sullivan and the Senecas* (2018), and *1780: Year of Revenge* (2019), all published by Sunbury Press Inc.

Against the Ice is the author's twelfth non-fiction book about early Pennsylvania. Sunbury Press also published the eight non-fiction books in Moore's Frontier Pennsylvania Series in 2014.

Moore has participated in several archaeological excavations of Native American sites. These include the Village of Nain in Bethlehem, Pa.; the City Island project in Harrisburg, Pa., conducted by the Pennsylvania Historical and Museum Commission; a Bloomsburg University dig in 1999 at a Native American site near Nescopeck, Pa.; and a 1963 excavation of the New Jersey State Museum along the Delaware River north of Worthington State Forest.

The author's 46-year newspaper career (1966-2012) included stints as a reporter for The Wall Street Journal;

as managing editor of The Sentinel at Lewistown, Pa.; as editorial page editor, city editor and managing editor of The Daily Item in Sunbury, and as editor of the Eastern Pennsylvania Business Journal in Bethlehem, Pa. He was also a Harrisburg correspondent for Ottaway Newspapers in the early 1970s.

A professional storyteller, Moore specializes in historically accurate stories about early Pennsylvanians. Wearing 18th century-style clothing, he often appears in the persona of Susquehanna Jack.

For information about the author's storytelling programs and books, please contact:

John L. Moore
552 Queen Street
Northumberland, Pa. 17857
Telephone (570) 473-9803
Email: tomahawks1756@gmail.com

FRONTIER PENNSYLVANIA SERIES

Bows, Bullets, and Bears
JOHN L. MOORE

Warriors, Wampum, and Wolves
JOHN L. MOORE

Rivers, Raiders, and Renegades
JOHN L. MOORE

Cannons, Cattle, and Campfires
JOHN L. MOORE

Frontier Pennsylvania Series

Pioneers, Prisoners, and Peace Pipes
JOHN L. MOORE

Settlers, Soldiers, and Scalps
JOHN L. MOORE

Traders, Travelers, and Tomahawks
JOHN L. MOORE

Forts, Forests, and Flintlocks
JOHN L. MOORE

The story of **General Peter Muhlenberg**, born in Trappe, Pennsylvania, and minister in Woodstock, Virginia. He followed Washington throughout the Revolution, all the way to Yorktown where he charged the redoubt with Hamilton.

by Edward W. Hocker,
with contributions from Lawrence Knorr
DISTELFINK PRESS
Trade Paperback - 6 x 9 x 1
9781620062982
190 pages indexed
BIOGRAPHY & AUTOBIOGRAPHY / Military
HISTORY / United States / Revolutionary Period (1775-1800)
HISTORY / US History / Mid-Atlantic
PRICE: $16.95   wherever books are sold

www.ingramcontent.com/pod-product-compliance
Lightning Source LLC
Chambersburg PA
CBHW020009050426
42450CB00005B/382